CUBAN AMERICANS

By Raúl Galván

Marshall Cavendish
New York • London • Toronto

Published by
Marshall Cavendish Corporation
2415 Jerusalem Avenue
P.O. Box 587
North Bellmore, New York 11710, U.S.A.

Edited, designed, and produced by Water Buffalo Books, Milwaukee

Project director: Mark Sachner
Art director: Sabine Beaupré
Picture researcher: Diane Laska
Editorial: Valerie Weber
Cover design: Lee Goldstein
Marshall Cavendish development editor: MaryLee Knowlton
Marshall Cavendish editorial director: Evelyn Fazio

The author and editors would like to gratefully acknowledge the following for their help in the creation of this book: Dr. Rodolfo Cortina, Olga and Donald Llopis and family, Olga Ramos, Vicente Cossio, Arsenio Arza, Hilario Candela, Marta Alday, Blanca E. Colomina, and Daisy Cubías.

Picture Credits: © B. Bachmann/Camerique: 52; Sabine Beaupré 1994: 7, 17; © The Bettmann Archive: 64; © Hazel Hankin: 4, 50; © David C. Phillips: Cover, 1, 5, 19, 23 (both), 24 (both), 25, 28, 29, 32, 34, 35 (both), 39, 42, 44, 45, 46, 47, 48, 55, 56, 57, 58, 62, 65, 69 (bottom), 72; © Reuters/Bettmann: 53, 60, 67, 71; © UPI/Bettmann: 8, 10, 13, 14 (both), 16, 22, 26, 27, 31, 36, 37, 38, 40, 43, 63, 66 (both), 68 (both), 69 (top), 70, 73, 74; © William Werner: 6, 9, 12

Library of Congress Cataloging-in-Publication Data

Galván, Raúl.
    Cuban Americans / Raúl Galván.
      p.   cm. — (Cultures of America)
    Includes bibliographical references and index.
    ISBN 1-85435-780-8 (set). — ISBN 1-85435-786-7 :
    1. Cuban Americans—Juvenile literature. I. Title. II. Series.
    E184.C97G35   1994
    305.868'7291073—dc20   94-12605
                                         CIP
                                         AC

To PS – MS
Tuty, Beck, and Sara, this is for you and yours; learn and enjoy! – RG

Printed and bound in the U.S.A.

CONTENTS

INTRODUCTION

The year was 1959. The United States was enjoying the prosperity of the post-World War II era, and Dwight Eisenhower was in the middle of his term as the thirty-fourth president of the U.S. In Cuba, dictator Fulgencio Batista was fleeing Havana, after hosting his 1958 New Year's Eve Party. Batista was leaving the island he had ruled since 1952, driven out by an idealistic group of guerrilla fighters from the "26th of July" movement led by a young Cuban lawyer, Fidel Castro. Castro, who took power after Batista's escape, would send hundreds of thousands of Cubans fleeing the country. These Cubans felt that life as they had known it was about to come to an end and were concerned with the political direction in which their country was headed. The majority of them would end up in the United States — becoming the core of the group called Cuban Americans.

Newcomers to a nation that already had a substantial Spanish-speaking population, Cuban Americans would cherish their identity as *los Cubanos* even as they created a place for themselves in American society. They did not know it then, but they were on the verge of forming one of North America's most visible, energetic, and successful ethnic groups.

These Cuban youngsters are framed by a doorway in Havana, Cuba's capital and largest city.

CHAPTER ONE

LEAVING A HOMELAND
LIFE IN THE HOME COUNTRY

He was your typical all-Cuban boy. He lived in an apartment with his parents in the part of Havana called El Vedado and was in fifth grade at an all-boys Catholic school called De La Salle.

Pepito was much like many of the youngsters who later made the over one hundred-mile trip to Miami in the years after 1961. Nine years old, he lived comfortably in Havana, his family part of Cuba's growing middle class. His dad worked for an American paper manufacturing company, and his mom was a stay-at-home mom like June Cleaver, the Beaver's mom in the "Leave It to Beaver" TV series.

He lived in Cuba's largest city, rode in the family's Chevrolet to visit grandma, and played Cuba's favorite sport — *el beisbol* (baseball). And like many American youngsters, he dreamed of playing in the big leagues in America — the *Grandes Ligas*. He chewed Chiclets, brushed his teeth with Colgate toothpaste, and watched his favorite TV show, "El Llanero Solitario" ("The Lone Ranger"), with Spanish subtitles.

The times in the nation's capital were changing, however. Soldiers with machine guns were walking the streets on a regular basis. The trip to the beach outside Havana included a ride over mined bridges. And once at the beach, there was the company of

a tank buried in the ivory white sand, guarding against foreign invaders.

Pepito's mom had made him start taking English lessons in preparation for the trip to the United States and a move to Aunt Sara's in Miami. A new government had taken hold in Cuba, and Pepito's parents, unsure of what would happen on their island, were worried about the future of the republic.

Cuba in the Late 1950s

By Latin American standards, the Cuba about to be left behind by Pepito, and later his parents, was a growing and successful country. Spanish was its official language, and it was spoken fast. Cubans, always willing to

Most Cuban immigrants have come to the U.S. by way of Florida in four distinct "waves" that began in the late 1950s.

express themselves, chopped off the ends of words to speed up their delivery. And much like Ricky Ricardo, the Cuban character played by real-life Cuban Desi Arnaz in the television show "I Love Lucy," Cubans used the entire body to communicate. Roman Catholicism was the country's primary religion, yet Cubans' church attendance was low compared to that of North American Catholics. The island's population was estimated to be between 6 and 6.5 million Cubans, about 60 percent of whom lived in urban centers. Over a million lived in the metropolitan La Habana (Havana) area. Santiago, the second-largest city in the country, was populated by about 180,000 Cubans. The rest of the population lived in smaller cities and towns (forty-six of them with at least 8,000 people), with the poorest living in the countryside.

Ethnically, the population was mainly white and of European descent and about one-third of Black and African Cuban descent. Although racial discrimination ex-isted, most Cubans felt that it was not as widespread as in the U.S. In fact, the civil rights movement in Cuba dated back to 1940, when the newly drafted constitution barred all racial discrimination. What discrimination existed was much different from that in the States. It was based mainly on money and income, but since most Afro-Cubans were poor, it took on a racial tone as well. The actual skin tone of a Black person affected his or her social standing: The lighter the skin of a Black, the better the chance of his or her acceptance in society. In Cuba, there were no separate but equal facilities for whites and Blacks as there had been in the States, although there were unwritten understandings, especially in the Havana tourist centers, about where Blacks were not allowed. There was, however, no persecution of Blacks in Cuba as there had been in the American South.

Cuba enjoyed one of the highest standards of living in all of Latin America, even though its economy had not grown in some

The beach has long provided a background for many Cuban family gatherings. This family enjoys the beach at Playa Larga, near the site of the 1961 American-backed Bay of Pigs invasion.

A busy street in modern Havana. Many Cubans continue to drive automobiles manufactured in the United States in the 1950s, before the U.S. suspended trade with Cuban leader Fidel Castro.

time. Cuba's main export, sugar, was in top demand and could not possibly be sold to any more countries than already bought it. Most business people on the island were involved in the sugar industry. Cuba's tobacco crop was its number two export.

Tourism was developing as an industry during the 1950s. About 350,000 tourists had visited the island in 1957. In Havana, several new luxury hotels had been built in the fifties, among them the $14 million, thirty-story Havana Riviera Hotel and the Havana Hilton Hotel. These hotels and their casinos were frequented by American tourists. Not surprisingly, many of these tourists were members of American organized crime, attracted to Havana's freewheeling lifestyle, especially the high-stakes gambling of the Las Vegas of Latin America.

Life in the Old Country

The island of Cuba stretches out from west to east, roughly 750 miles wide. Its land is relatively flat, except for the eastern quarter of the island, where the terrain is mountainous and there's a range of mountains called the Sierra Maestra. The western quarter of the island features smaller hills and valleys. The capital, Havana, lies on the northern coast of the island, ninety miles south of Key West, Florida.

The Cuban people of the fifties were grouped into somewhat similar classifications as their North American neighbors. Cuba had a small and elite wealthy class. At the other end of the social scale were about two hundred thousand families of peasants and an additional six hundred thousand rural workers who lived in poverty for most of the year with little or no education and even less medical attention. Close to half of the doctors on the island lived and worked in Havana, making health care difficult to obtain in the rural areas. For this group of poverty-stricken Cubans, the future promised little hope.

As mentioned earlier, Cuba had a large middle class population compared to other Latin American countries, somewhere between 25 and 33 percent of the population. Like Pepito and his parents, most of the Cubans who made up the émigré group that began to land in Miami in 1959 came from the upper and middle classes.

Although Cuba was better off than other countries in Latin America, based on income per person, and people were not starving, there was widespread poverty on the island, a poverty caused by an unequal sharing of wealth. The wealthiest 20 percent of the population controlled 60 percent of the income. Unemployment was usually close to 30 percent, and for hundreds of thousands of Cubans, employment meant cutting sugar cane, a job that lasted from four to six months every year.

By the 1950s, the literacy rate was estimated to be 67 percent — much higher than in other countries in Latin America. The constitution of 1940 had made education compulsory for children between six and fourteen years of age. In 1953, however, only 40 percent of all children actually attended elementary school. At fourteen, they could go on to the seventh and eighth grades. It's estimated that only 30 percent of Havana's teenage population and 7 percent of the rural teenagers attended high school.

Public schools were managed poorly, and some parents sent their children to private religious schools, such as Pepito's De La Salle, which was operated by the Christian Brothers, and the Jesuit Belén School, which Fidel Castro attended. It was generally believed that the Catholic schools and even many English-speaking schools offered a better education than the public schools. Children who didn't go to school spent their days on the street — running errands, carrying baskets, and collecting garbage.

Street vendors sell tropical fruit in front of the Malecon, Havana's seafront boulevard.

CUBA AND THE U.S.: LINKED IN THE PAST

Cuba, the Pearl of the Antilles, had been the anchor of the Spanish Empire in the Western Hemisphere since Christopher Columbus landed on its eastern coast in 1492. The Spanish colonized and ruled Cuba much as the British would later colonize the eastern part of North America. In 1898, Cuba achieved independence from Spain.

Because it is so close to the United States and because of American involvement in the Cuban independence struggle, Cuba had always had close ties to the United States. In 1898, the U.S. sent the military ship *Maine* to Cuba to protect Americans living there. When the ship blew up in the Havana harbor, the Spanish were blamed for the explosion, and the U.S. declared war on Spain.

After a few weeks of serious fighting, Spain and the U.S. agreed to peace, and the Cuban people were on their way to self-rule — or so they thought. U.S. President William McKinley, however, was not prepared to accept a Cuban government ruled by Cuban revolutionaries and established military rule on the island for the next four years.

Although the great Cuban migration to the States began in 1959, Cubans had been living in the U.S. as early as the 1820s. They later came in larger numbers in the 1870s to work in the cigar industry, with the largest concentrations of Cubans located in Key West and Tampa, Florida. Cubans had also traditionally found refuge in the U.S. during times of political instability on the island or when fleeing political oppression.

In fact, José Martí, the Cuban hero who would lead the effort in the battle with Spain, had found refuge in New York in 1875 at the age of twenty-two. Martí later spearheaded the Cuban uprising against Spain and traveled the United States, raising money to pay for the fight that would give birth to the Cuban republic. Three decades later, in the 1930s, during the Gerardo Machado regime, Cubans again began to flee the island, with Miami serving as the primary destination of choice in the States.

Life in Havana, Cuba's Largest City

The city of Havana was home to one-sixth of the island's population. Housing in the city included a mix of houses and apartments that would seem normal to a city dweller in North America, and life in Havana was like life in many big North American cities. The Cuban middle class had always kept up with and imitated American popular culture. Television had come to Cuba in a big way — with nearly five hundred thousand sets on the island, all American made. There were also more than a million radios in use. North American music received lots of play on the airwaves, as did subtitled or dubbed U.S. television programs. Havana was also the first city in the world to have an automated telephone system. In fact, the Cuban American Telephone and Telegraph Company was owned in great part by International Telephone and Telegraph, an American company. Most cars on the island (many of them still running today) were also American. The Cuban *peso* and U.S. dollar were interchangeable, and American-made products found a ready and eager market in Cuba.

As in the United States, baseball was the

A typical country dwelling in Cuba. Many houses in tropical Cuba have roofs that are made out of palm leaves.

national pastime. Many Cubans played in the U.S. major leagues during the summer and returned to the island in the winter to play in the Cuban Winter League for one of the league's four teams. But unlike the United States, which had only recently allowed African Americans into the major leagues, Cuba had long welcomed Black ball players, many from the States. While baseball was Cuba's main spectator sport, boxing was also very popular. Havana was the country's center of culture, with many social clubs and a spectacular nightlife featuring "the largest nightclub in the world" — the Tropicana.

Everyday Life in Cuba

Most Cubans typically ate two meals a day — lunch and dinner — with dinner usually taking place much later than the traditional North American supper. The Cuban diet often included beef and pork, as well as fresh fish. A typical meal consisted of black beans and rice, roast pork, and one of the many tropical vegetables grown in Cuba, such as plantains (a relative of the banana), *boniato* (sweet potatoes), *malanga* (a potatolike root), and *yuca* (cassava). The plantains were typically fried in lard or oil, while the boniato, malanga, and yuca were boiled in water until soft. Malanga and yuca were usually served with *mojo,* a light sauce made of lemon juice and oil.

Coca-Cola, Pepsi-Cola, and Canada Dry were all typical beverages on the island, as were local fruit drinks, often made on the street. Another delicacy available on the streets were *churros,* deep-fried sticks of dough coated with sugar. Long popular with

Cuban Americans in Miami, churros are now available at many sports stadiums throughout the United States.

About a quarter of the houses in Cuba were built of masonry and cement, with most found in the cities. In the country, the wealthy farmers and sugar growers were used to lots of room. Most lived in large farmsteads, which were far from their neighboring towns, while the peasants lived in the traditional Cuban country dwellings called *bohíos.* The bohío was a one-room dwelling made of wood with palm leaf roofs and earthen floors.

From Cuba to the United States

The largest migration of Cubans to the States, which began in the late 1950s, took place in four distinct waves, or groups of immigration. The first wave, which began to arrive in Miami in late 1958 and early 1959, was made up mostly of members of the Fulgencia Batista government. The first stage of this wave numbered about three thousand people. The *Batistianos,* as they were called, left the island immediately for fear they would be imprisoned by the newly installed Castro government. Many of them had fought against Castro's army during the revolution.

Pepito's case was similar to that of many other kids and their families. His parents were afraid of and uncomfortable with the political direction of the Castro revolution, so they applied for a visa, or permission, for Pepito to come to the United States. Pepito's parents were concerned that they wouldn't be allowed to raise their son in the manner they wished since it was rumored that kids would be sent to boarding schools around Cuba and would only be allowed to spend a limited time with their parents. His parents were also concerned that, under the new

A thirty-three-year-old Fidel Castro leads his forces during his 1959 victory march into Havana.

government, they wouldn't be allowed to express their opinions. After waiting for several months, the visa finally arrived, and Pepito was on his way to Miami to live with Aunt Sara. Months later, Pepito's mother left Havana, and within a year, Pepito's family was back together when his dad arrived in Miami.

The first wave of Cuban immigrants continued to arrive on regularly scheduled flights, but in 1962, those flights came to a halt during a face-off between the U.S. and the Soviet Union over the placement of Soviet missiles in nearby Cuba. Following this tense confrontation, known in the U.S. as the Cuban missile crisis, Cuban citizens were forbidden to emigrate from their island.

During the first wave of Cuban migra-

A Cuban woman and her son are greeted by her other children upon arrival in Miami in 1961.

tion, a total of about 280,000 Cubans arrived in the United States, most of them white, middle aged and well educated. Only 4 percent of the immigrants had less than a fourth-grade education. This group would become one of America's most economically productive refugee groups. In 1965, the second wave of migration got underway when the U.S. began a government-sponsored airlift. This wave lasted until 1973 and brought an additional 273,000 Cubans to the States. Most of these second-wave immigrants were also middle aged, educated, and of white European descent.

The third wave of Cuban migration was set off between April and September of 1980, when 125,000 Cubans entered the United States. Their port of departure from Cuba was Mariel, and the new

A boat of *Marielitos* arrives in Key West in 1980. Most of the boat's passengers were single men, as were many in the third wave of immigrants to arrive from Cuba.

group of émigrés was dubbed "the *Marielitos*" (those from Mariel).

Over the course of these three waves, Cubans spread throughout all U.S. social classes. It has been estimated that 10 percent of them earned over $45,000 a year and that about an additional 50 percent made up a Cuban American middle class. The remaining 40 percent had incomes below the poverty line.

The fourth wave is the most recent of Cubans to migrate to the States. With the collapse of the Soviet Union and the elimination of Soviet aid, Cuba found itself with a decreasing supply of fuel oil, food, clothing, and other goods, and the Cuban government began to ease travel restrictions abroad. Many Cubans have used home-built rafts or *balsas,* made up of large inner tubes, as a way of escape. During the early 1990s, they continued to arrive on Florida's shores at alarming rates as the Cuban economy continued to worsen. This group of immigrants, named after the crafts they sailed to the States, are called *balseros,* or raft people. Defections of Cubans to other countries also continued, among them nearly forty athletes from the Cuban delegation to the Central American and Caribbean games in Puerto Rico who stayed behind in December of 1993. Later that month, even Fidel Castro's daughter emigrated to the United States.

All in all, it is estimated that over a million Cuban Americans live in the United States. As you will read in the next chapter, Cuban Americans have re-created Cuba in Miami, many of them prospering and succeeding, while continuing to retain their Cuban roots.

MARIELITOS: A NEW WAVE OF EXILES

In April of 1980, thousands of Cubans invaded the Peruvian embassy in Havana seeking asylum. Castro decided to allow these people and others he called undesirables to leave the country. In order to leave, however, these Cubans and many others were forced to travel to the port city of Mariel to board a fleet of boats that had come from the United States to pick them up.

These Marielitos were a much different group than the Cubans of the first two waves. Castro emptied his prisons and mental institutions, sending political prisoners and criminals, as well as people who were mentally ill, along with the other Cubans who had chosen to leave. Unlike the first and second waves of Cuban immigrants, which were made up of families, the Marielitos consisted of mainly single males and females, and about 12 percent were homosexuals. In addition to sending over so many people who were outside of the mainstream of Cuban society, Castro reportedly even shipped over a number of Cuban spies.

Upon arriving in the Florida Keys, these Cubans were processed and sent to Cuban resettlement camps throughout the U.S. to await sponsorship by families and friends. Eventually, most Cubans found sponsors and made their way to Miami, where they were not warmly received by many of their fellow Cuban Americans. The hard-core criminals were transferred to American prisons, with the largest group going to the Atlanta Federal Penitentiary in Georgia.

A happy reunion at the Miami airport in October of 1960. The man had escaped Cuba, along with twenty others, in a boat that landed in Key West.

CHAPTER TWO

LIFE IN A NEW LAND
A WORLD NINETY MILES AWAY

Cubans began leaving their island in significant numbers in 1959. Like thousands of Cubans who made the short trip to the States, Pepito ended up in Miami in 1961, only ninety miles from Cuba, though he would later move to the Midwest. And as often happened with other ethnic groups who settle in the United States, the Cubans brought their culture, language, food, and music to Miami, eventually turning the city into a bustling community, a gateway to Latin America. Most came directly from Cuba, but others found their way out of Cuba through a third country, often Spain or Mexico. Those who came directly from Cuba were given refugee status by the Immigration and Naturalization Service (INS), gaining immediate legal entry into the United States. Those entering from other countries, however, came into the country as aliens and found themselves subject to INS laws, which delayed their entry by a year or more.

Life in Miami

The Miami that Cubans encountered was best known as the city next to Miami Beach, a popular American tourist destination of the 1950s. In 1960, Miami was

● Counties with Cuban American population over 10,000 (1980)

Most Cubans who immigrated landed in Miami. From there, many were relocated to other parts of the U.S. Union City, New Jersey, attracted the largest number of Cubans who headed north.

primarily a white, Anglo community, with 81 percent of its population fitting that description, 15 percent of the population African American, and only 4 percent Latin.

It has been estimated that there were between 10,000 and 12,000 Cubans living in Miami before the first wave of immigration began. From New Year's Day of 1959, however, when Castro took power, to June 30, 1960, more than 26,500 Cubans came to the United States, escaping a form of government that was quickly becoming socialist and had begun to limit personal freedoms.

By October 1962, it is estimated that over 150,000 Cubans had entered the United States, mostly through Miami. Over 13,000 of the Cuban émigrés were children who were sent alone to the States by their parents. They often ended up in American orphanages and foster homes through the efforts of groups such as *Operación Pedro Pan* (Operation Peter Pan).

Most Cubans arrived by plane in the sixties, with a small minority making the trip by boat and even on homemade rafts. Those who did not stay in Miami continued their journeys north by train, car, and bus.

Miami was very similar to the cities they had left behind. The climate was much the same, with summer temperatures between eighty and ninety degrees. Geographically, it was much like Cuba. It was relatively flat, and the vegetation was similar, with many palm and fruit trees. The architecture was also like Cuba's, with heavy use of masonry construction, tile roofs, and modern design. And almost instantly, the foods familiar to Cubans in Cuba became available at Cuban groceries in Miami. Carts in the streets also sold Cuban food, and cafeterias with windows facing the sidewalk offered Cubans the chance to stop for a *pastelito*, a Cuban pastry filled with meat or tropical fruit, washed down by a hearty *cafecito*, a Cuban espresso drunk in small but potent servings.

But while the environment was familiar, the people, language, and culture the Cubans encountered were different. English replaced the familiar Spanish as the dominant language, and there were cultural differences

OPERACIÓN PEDRO PAN

On January 9, 1961, the U.S. State Department gave Monsignor Bryan Walsh of the Miami archdiocese the authority to give visa waivers to Cuban children from six to sixteen years of age. In doing so, the Unaccompanied Children's Program of the Diocese of Miami was born. The program was also referred to as *Operación Pedro Pan,* named after the popular Disney character. The program was developed as a response to rumors circulating in Miami that Castro would soon send Cuban kids to work on Soviet farms, and later that all children ages three to ten would be sent to live in state-sponsored dormitories, where they would be allowed to see their parents only two days a month.

Many parents, frightened for their children, sent them by themselves to live in six camps in the United States under the guardianship of the Diocese of Miami. The last of these camps did not close until 1981. Between January 1961, when the program was started, until September 1963, more than 14,000 children came to the United States under the Pedro Pan program.

between the Americans and the new immigrants. In terms of body language and speaking style, the Americans were more reserved than the loud and expressive Cubans. The Cubans were unfamiliar with the city, and housing was often smaller and not as nice as that in Cuba. While much of the environment was the same, the Cubans were still in a foreign country.

As Cubans streamed into Miami, many settled in the area of Miami now referred to as Little Havana, an area roughly four square miles located southwest of the central business district and intersected by SW Eighth Street, or *La Calle Ocho,* as it came to be known. Once a prosperous middle-class neighborhood, the area had become depressed and was losing population, therefore affording Cubans with plenty of low-cost housing.

Cubans arriving in Miami would typically live with family members or friends, often several families in a house, until they could get on their feet and find their own place to live. Pepito, like many other kids, arrived in Miami by himself and quickly found himself with Aunt Sara and two cousins. Those not fortunate enough to have families with whom to stay were able to find inexpensive hotel rooms, many of which were available in the declining tourist climate. Tourists, who in the forties and fifties had visited Miami Beach, were now instead starting to travel to Caribbean islands that were beginning to market their tourist industries.

The Cubans typically arrived in Miami carrying all their worldly possessions in a bag — often a large, military-type duffel bag in which they had packed a few changes of clothes, personal possessions of little value, and often a bottle of rum and a box of Cuban cigars. Around 87 percent of the arriving

Tropical fruit for sale in a Miami market.

Cubans came from Havana, Santiago, and other large cities and were therefore familiar with city life.

The common belief is that the majority of these Cubans were members of Cuba's elite class, but research has shown this to be incorrect. Nearly one-third were in clerical and sales positions, with only 22 percent being classified as professionals. The balance represented nearly every imaginable occupation. The professionals were without American certification in their professions: Doctors were unable work as doctors until they passed their medical board tests, and lawyers were unable to work as lawyers until they passed their bar examinations.

Most of the Cubans spoke little or no English, and jobs, particularly well-paying ones, were scarce. Some Cubans, particularly those who were able to get money out of the country before their exodus, started their own businesses. Other Cubans were forced to find whatever employment they could — washing dishes, mopping floors, even selling shoes door-to-door.

Although not fluent in English, the Cubans did not experience total culture shock; they were somewhat familiar with American life. Many had either visited the U.S. or had business contacts with the U.S., and most had bought and used American products in Cuba.

"Se cae Fidel." ("Fidel will fall.")

It's safe to say that most Cubans believed their stay in the U.S. would be a temporary

EL REFUGIO

In 1961, in order to help Cubans adjust to life in America, President John F. Kennedy established the Cuban Refugee Program. Headquartered at the aptly named Freedom Tower in downtown Miami, the program provided a job placement program and offered temporary financial assistance and other welfare benefits. Single Cubans qualified for a payment of sixty dollars, while families were given one hundred dollars a month until they found a job.

The Cuban Refugee Program was referred to as *El Refugio* (The Refuge) by the Cuban immigrants and provided them with a common starting point, much as Ellis Island had been the first stop for many European immigrants entering the U.S. through New York City earlier in the century. Cubans would register at the Freedom Tower, where among numerous activities they would undergo medical testing and even receive a Red Cross kit that consisted of a razor, two blades, two bandages, and a bottle of aspirin. A Cuban woman also recalled receiving a card that entitled her to free lunch and dinner for a week at a local restaurant.

As the Cubans continued to arrive in Miami, the already strained Miami economy was at a loss to provide opportunities to the incoming refugees. The Refugee Program then sought to relocate families out of Miami. Those with some ability to speak English and some education were offered opportunities to move north.

If they refused an offer to relocate, they were denied any further government assistance and were considered to be on their own. Of the nearly 495,000 Cubans who registered with the Cuban Refugee Program between 1961 and 1981, about 61 percent were resettled. Most of those eventually returned to Miami after they were able to save some money, get accustomed to life in the United States, and learn English. They returned to be with their families and friends and to partake in the Cuban culture of Miami.

Pepito's family was one of those resettled, helped by a Catholic relief organization that sponsored their move to a western Illinois community, where both his parents found employment at an agricultural equipment manufacturer. Cubans arriving in U.S. cities often acted as magnets for other Cubans living in Miami. Pepito's family eventually was able to get another Catholic parish in the same community to help lifelong friends come to their town. And before long, that family was also helping its relatives come to the same town.

one. They thought that when Fidel Castro's regime fell, they would be able to return to their beloved island. That was perhaps the biggest difference between the Cubans and any other immigrant group who had previously come to this country.

The hope, looking back now a false one, of returning to live in Cuba was eternal and influenced Cubans' lifestyles. It wasn't unusual to hear Cubans talk of their plans to return to the island and discuss the latest rumors of Castro's impending fall. In 1966, a survey in Miami indicated that 83 percent of the Cuban respondents would return to Cuba if the island were to become free. Likewise, it was typical to hear Cubans in Miami talking unfavorably of their new home, particularly as it compared to their homeland, while holding on fiercely to their Cuban identity in Miami and the other cities in which they had settled. To keep their hopes of returning to Cuba alive meant keeping their Cubanness alive. All agreed that the United States was a great country, one full of

opportunity, but one that could not offer the lifestyle they had left behind.

Early in their exile, several Cuban groups worked to overthrow Fidel Castro in Cuba, the best known being the 2506 Brigade, which was trained and supported by the U.S. Central Intelligence Agency (CIA). This group was part of the Bay of Pigs invasion in Cuba in 1961. Other groups, such as Omega 7 and Alpha 66, also advocated military force to overthrow Castro. These groups staged numerous operations to Cuba from the Florida Keys, landing small groups of guerrillas on the island. In this country, Omega 7 claimed responsibility for the January 1983 explosions at the office of *Replica* magazine, whose articles had implied support for a dialogue with Castro, and at a cigar factory owned by a Cuban. The Cuban had been photographed handing Castro one of his company's cigars during 1978 talks in Havana between Castro and Cuban American businessmen comprising the Committee of 75. In April 1979, a group calling itself *Comando Cero* had claimed

THE BAY OF PIGS INVASION

In early 1961, a military force made up of more than fourteen hundred exiled Cubans and several Americans, all trained by the Central Intelligence Agency (CIA), invaded Cuba. The force, which was named the 2506 Brigade, took off from Puerto Cabezas in Nicaragua and landed on the southern coast of Cuba in April 1961. They landed in the Bahia de Cochinos (Bay of Pigs) and were quickly fought by the Cuban army.

The plan was for the invading Cubans to land on the island and take control of a location where they would install a new Cuban government that had been organized

by Cubans in the United States. The new government would then be immediately recognized by the United States.

The invasion was a failure. One hundred fourteen brigade members were killed, and 1,189 of them were captured by the Cuban army. They were jailed and spent over a year in Cuban prisons before they were exchanged by Castro for $53 million worth of food and drugs in December of 1962.

A week later, the men and their families gathered at the Orange Bowl in Miami, where a member of the 2506 Brigade handed the brigade's flag to President Kennedy.

A veteran of the exile 2506 Brigade stands at attention during the playing of the Cuban National Anthem during a ceremony in Miami on April 17, 1986, commemorating the twenty-fifth anniversary of the 1981 Bay of Pigs invasion.

credit for the murder of a man who had participated in talks with Castro, and in November of 1979, another participant of these talks was gunned down in Union City, New Jersey. The actions of these militant groups were not condoned by the majority of Cuban Americans in Miami.

Cubans Move North

While Miami was the primary destination of most Cubans, some continued north to join family members while others were resettled. The most popular destinations were New York City and Union City, New Jersey. These areas had been traditional destinations of earlier Cubans and offered them employment opportunities not available in Miami. Other significant numbers of Cubans relocated to Chicago and Los Angeles.

Unlike Miami, which provided the Cubans with a city with similar climate and architecture, Union City presented an additional challenge — the environment. The Cubans, accustomed to living in tropical temperatures, were suddenly thrust into an American city with cold temperatures, snow, ice, and, in the winter, early sunsets. The economy in Union City, however, offered the Cubans work in factories and manufacturing plants where the ability to speak English was not important.

While Miami and Union City housed the majority of all Cubans in the States, many Cubans were relocated to smaller cities throughout the United States. These families and individuals were thrust into lives totally unlike their previous ones. Unlike their brothers and sisters in Union City and even Chicago or Los Angeles, these Cubans were without the support of their own compatriots and were often the only non-Anglos in their neighborhood. Those with a poor grasp of the English language were forced into work as laborers, while those who spoke English often worked in jobs that involved the Spanish language, such as teaching Spanish, translating, or working in import and export businesses.

The Cuban American children attended schools that didn't offer bilingual education programs, so initially they often felt like outsiders in their own classrooms, unable to understand the teachers or their classmates. In a short time, however, most were forced to learn English and were able to integrate themselves into school life. Those who stayed in the North often married Americans and began their assimilation into mainstream America much more quickly than their Miami cousins. Pepito was one of these young Cubans; he made his assimilation smoothly but now, more than ever, holds on to his Cuban identity in spite of living in a city with little Cuban culture.

The Adventurous Cubans

Facing the reality of life in a foreign country, lacking the ability to speak English, and lacking employment opportunities in Miami, Cubans turned to each other. The Miami they entered was a city in hard financial times. In the central city area around Eighth Street, more than one thousand houses that had been financed partly by the government had been vacated, and many were being vandalized. Shops were closing, and downtown establishments were suffering.

Using limited amounts of money, primarily coming from meager savings, and working long hours, often on multiple jobs, the Cubans turned Miami into a thriving economy in just a decade. In spite of the influx of an additional 125,000 Cubans (the

Cuban American businesses, many of them restaurants, dot the Miami landscape. This proud restaurateur shows off a *lechón asado* (roasted suckling pig) and a *paella*, a Cuban version of the traditional Spanish dish.

Among the many Cuban American businesses re-created in Miami is the Cawy Bottling Company. Vicente Cossío, pictured here holding a can of Cawy's best, is the company president.

The Versailles Restaurant, a Cuban American landmark on Miami's Calle Ocho.

Roberto Aguilera, assistant manager of the Versailles Restaurant, chats with Arsenio Arza, sales manager for the Cawy Bottling Company.

Marielitos) and tens of thousands of Haitian and Central American immigrants, Florida in 1982 still had one of the lowest unemployment rates in the U.S. Dade County, the county in which Miami is located, with a 6.8 percent figure, had the lowest unemployment rate in Florida. By the early 1980s, Cuban households in Florida had higher incomes than those of most other Floridians.

There were at least two hundred millionaires among the thousands of successful Cuban business people. These included Felipe Valls, who began washing dishes in Miami, found a job as a salesman in a restaurant supply company, and eventually owned five restaurants, including the successful Versailles Restaurant in Miami. In 1981, Valls's five restaurants grossed $6 million in sales.

Armando Codina was one of the Operación Pedro Pan children who went to live with a foster family in New Jersey as a

Cuban American-owned supermarkets have sprung up throughout Miami. This Sedano's store is on Miami's Flagler Street.

thirteen-year-old. After returning to Florida in 1967 to meet his mother, who had arrived from Cuba, and after finishing high school, he was hired by a Jacksonville, Florida, bank as a messenger and worked nights as a bag boy at a local grocery store.

He was eventually promoted to teller at the bank and became proficient with computers. After two years, he moved to Miami with his mother to become a loan officer. Eventually, he created a computer software firm that he sold in 1978 for between $3 and $4 million.

José Pineiro invested his last dollars in some secondhand records and began to sell them door-to-door. He saved his profits from a month and opened a small store from which he began selling imports. He eventually opened several other record stores throughout the Miami area and by 1983 had become a distributor of Latin American music throughout the United States.

Amaury Betancourt, who was hired as a clerk at a Miami bank in 1961, became president and chairman of one of Miami's Cuban-owned banks. In 1982, he retired with bank assets valued at about $120 million.

In achieving their personal success, these Cuban entrepreneurs, along with many of the other eighteen thousand Cuban business owners in Miami, established a Cuban business community that provided employment, as well as products and services, to their fellow Cubans. In 1983, it was estimated that Cuban Americans accounted for about twenty-five thousand of Miami's garment workers, half the aircraft repair and maintenance labor force in Dade County, as well as over thirty-five hundred doctors and over five hundred lawyers. There were sixteen Cuban American bank presidents, and Cubans owned over sixty car dealerships, about five hundred supermarkets, and close to 250 drugstores.

Across the country, Cuban Americans enjoyed success in a number of fields ranging from education to high technology. A young chemist working with the Havana Coca-Cola bottling plant left Cuba in 1960 and ended up in the Nassau, Bahamas, Coca-Cola plant. Twenty-one years later, he had risen through the corporate ranks to become Coca-Cola's chairman and chief executive officer. We'll meet Roberto Goizueta and other heroes in Cuban American success stories in Chapter Six.

Facing Discrimination

Like most immigrants who have come to the U.S. during its history, the Cubans, too, encountered a certain degree of discrimination that displayed itself most often when Cubans looked for housing. Perhaps because the overwhelming majority of the early immigrants were white, discrimination took on a social and cultural tone. A woman who came to Miami in 1962 talked about her search for an apartment and told of the sign she saw at one location: No dogs, no Latins.

As Cuban Americans became entrenched in Miami and elsewhere, they felt that they were pretty much able to achieve whatever they wished for themselves and their children. They seemed willing to accept the prejudice they faced as part of the immigrant experience and chose to look upon the offenders as ignorant or unworldly.

The number of Afro-Cubans increased in the second and third waves of Cuban migration, and Cuban Blacks experienced the phenomenon of racial discrimination in the States. Ironically, many of the Marielitos, members of the third wave of migration, faced difficult times after settling in Miami in the early eighties. The feeling among the earlier Cuban settlers was that this group of Cubans, with its large number of prisoners and other people from the margins of Cuban society, was "too different." The early Cubans saw the Marielitos as a threat to the reputation they had already

Participants in a 1987 rebellion of Cuban inmates at the Atlanta Federal Penitentiary are led out of the prison. The Marielitos were protesting their proposed return to Cuba.

The wife of one of the Cuban inmates in the Atlanta Penitentiary fears her husband may have been hurt during the 1987 revolt.

established. These Cubans suffered a certain amount of discrimination at the hands of their fellow Cubans but were eventually accepted into the Cuban American community in Miami.

The Cuban Americans Assimilate

It would be difficult to say that the Cubans of the first generation have fully assimilated into American life. However, Cubans who came to this country as teens or younger are well on their way to life as Americans, particularly those who grew up outside of the Miami Cuban experience.

Even in Miami, this group of Cuban Americans settled into what could be considered the American way of life, with some of the amenities of old Cuba, such as Cuban food, social clubs, family get-togethers, and Spanish-language media. In the late eighties, Miami even elected its first Cuban-born mayor — Xavier Suarez, at the time one of the few Cuban American politicians whose political platform was not based primarily on anti-Castro themes. As we'll see in the coming chapters, Cuban life is thriving in Miami, allowing Cuban Americans to enjoy the best of both Cuban and American cultures.

The hope of most Cuban Americans today is not of returning to Cuba but of attaining financial security for themselves and their children here in the United States. Now, instead of dreaming about their return to the island, they've accepted America as theirs. The Cuban Americans have become American citizens, while retaining their roots. And in Miami, they've helped create the country's most culturally diverse city.

27

The mother is a highly respected and protected member of the Cuban family. Here, mother and daughter celebrate Mother's Day in Miami.

CHAPTER THREE

FAMILY AND COMMUNITY
THE GREATER CUBAN AMERICAN FAMILY

A large part of the success experienced by the Cuban American community in the United States has been helped by the support given by the family, a family that has traditionally been very close-knit. But the idea of "family" for Cuban Americans also encompasses the extended family, which includes relatives and friends. All of these people are part of the greater Cuban family. In order to better understand the Cuban family structure, it's important to know the roles of the individuals who make up that family, in particular the roles of the male and female.

The Traditional Cuban Family

As had been the case historically in much of Latin America, and to a smaller extent today, the Cuban male was the unquestioned head of the family unit. And like many other Latin males, he was exposed to the tradition of *machismo*. Machismo is a concept common in Latin America. It allows men to express their virility through physical strength, demonstrations of courage, and in some cases, success in business.

Men and Women in Cuba. As it related to family dynamics, the Cuban father's ma-

Sister and brother cool off on a hot Miami afternoon. Family gatherings are frequent and usually include cousins and other family members and friends.

chismo was expressed in a variety of ways. Fathers protected their daughters by watching over them intensely. For example, they would not allow them to date without the company of a family-assigned chaperone. Under the principles of machismo, young men were allowed to have sexual liberties, but young women were expected to remain virgins until their wedding day.

As patriarch, the father was also given the right to exercise authority over the females of the family, who, in most cases, did not work outside the home. Machismo, as did Latin culture in general, stressed that a woman's place was in the home, taking care of and raising the kids. Because of the male dominance in the family unit, the male had most, if not all, of the say in most decisions, leaving the woman in a position of weakness, to be revered but also protected.

Family: The Main Source of Pride. Above all, however, the identity of the family was a source of pride for males and females alike — so much, in fact, that in order to acknowledge family identity, Latin children would traditionally accept both their father's and their mother's surnames. Pepito Garcia Martinez thus was the son of the father Garcia and of the mother Martinez. Following tradition, Mrs. Martinez, Pepito's mother, retained her maiden name but, according to custom, added de Garcia (of Garcia) to her name, becoming Clara Martinez de Garcia.

The family unit often also included grandma and grandpa or another aunt or uncle who lived with the family, creating a sort of living family tree. Grandma and grandpa were to be treated respectfully and revered for their wisdom and dominance over the rest of the family. Often the grandparents would live in the same house as the rest of the family until their death, since the concept of placing senior citizens in nursing homes was not accepted in Cuban culture or in Latin American culture generally.

As time passed, however, and the families moved to the United States, the traditions began to change, making the Cuban American experience vary from that of other Latin American cultures. "¿Que Pasa, USA?," a Cuban television program produced in Miami in the eighties featuring the life of a Cuban American family in Miami, used the extended family unit to create conflict and humor. The generation gap was quite clear as the Spanish-speaking grandmother and grandfather attempted to communicate with teenage grandchildren who wanted only to speak in English and act like Anglo teenagers, much to the frustration of their grandparents.

The Cuban Family in the United States

Once in the U.S., the family power structure began to change. Many men found it difficult to find jobs. In order for families to survive, the woman in the family was often faced with the challenge of finding a job — and often did so before the husband. Some were employed for the first time in their lives. Many women found jobs as garment workers in the clothing industry, which grew from seven thousand workers in 1964 to twenty-four thousand in 1973. In 1980, a study indicated that slightly more than 50 percent of all Cuban American women over sixteen years of age worked outside the home, while another study indicated that fewer than one-fourth of the women in Cuba worked before coming to the States.

With Cuban women going outside the home to work, the concept of machismo began to change. Middle-class Cuban American women, much like their Anglo counterparts, were forced into making the same tough decisions, choosing between being a stay-at-home mom and an employed mom. For Miriam Angulo, a bank senior vice president and later chief financial officer, the struggle to balance her role as a mother with her career led her to quit her bank job and start her own consulting firm — a move that would give her more time to raise her kids. And advertising executive Teresa Zubizarreta's decision to create her own agency was her way of keeping some control over her life and making the time to be with her children.

Out of Cuba:
Separation and Reunion

As the exodus from Cuba continued, many family members were often separated from one another. Some families were apart for periods of up to a year, others for longer periods of time — with the separation becoming permanent. Two Cuban-born brothers who were relocated to Arizona without their parents and lived with an American foster family never saw their father again; he died in Cuba. They were later reunited with their mother and grandmother, whom they helped support from the time they were teenagers. Other family members struggled financially to save money to send for relatives in Cuba as well as other countries, in times when they were barely making enough to feed themselves.

High school and college-aged youths were often forced to make a choice between school and work. If the family was struggling financially, the teenager would often go to work to help support the family, much like Armando Codina, the bank messenger from Chapter Two who went to live with his mother in

Reunited after years apart, a fifty-three-year old Cuban man is embraced by happy family members. The man and sixteen companions were picked up by U.S. authorities at sea between Cuba and the United States in the Straits of Florida during the Mariel boatlift in 1980.

Cuban American students take a lunch break with friends at Miami Senior High.

Jacksonville, Florida, on her arrival from Cuba in the early sixties.

As the families reunited, the parents and grandparents struggled to learn the English language and American culture. But the children, who tended to become more proficient with English sooner than their parents and grandparents, became the family's representatives, translators, and advisors in public and helped teach their parents about American institutions.

Assimilation Creates Conflict

In any immigrant group, it's common for the young first-generation and second-generation members to be the first to assimilate, or become familiar with the country in which they settle. The Cuban immigrants were no exception. But their quick assimilation also created problems for the Cuban families, as the young Cubans encountered value conflicts with their parents and grandparents.

The most common example revolved around the issue of dating. American teenagers could date without adult supervision, but in Cuban culture, it was not accepted for young ladies to date without a chaperone. Another source of conflict between Cuban American parents and their children was the wish of parents that their children be dependent on them, often late into their teens and even their twenties. Young adults, however, tended to drift toward the lifestyle of their Anglo friends, which offered more independence from the parents.

It's not surprising that many Cuban youngsters complained to their parents that they often felt both Cuban and American, or worse yet, neither Cuban nor American. They felt that their parents' Cuban values and rules were old-fashioned, yet while at home they had to live by those rules. Outside the home, however, life in school and among friends tended to be modeled after American values, or even after the characters in American movies or on American TV. Needless to say, these values often conflicted with mom and dad's ideas at home.

Seventeen years after arriving in the United States and now a father living in the American Midwest, Pepito tells a story about a late-night experience with his baby daughter. Pepito had vowed that he would speak to his children in Spanish as they grew up, with the idea of raising them to be bilingual. But late one night, in the baby's room for her midnight feeding, Pepito found it odd to be talking to a baby in Spanish while outside the window, the wind howled and the thermometer rested at below zero. The language, lifestyle, and culture of tropical Cuba were in conflict with the icy environment. And even in balmy Miami, many Cubans were moving out of Little Havana and into the suburbs,

further removing themselves from Cuban culture.

As the Cuban second generation has grown older, studies have shown that its members have assimilated into the American mainstream more fully than their parents. Much of this has been caused by a higher number of marriages between Cubans and Anglos. According to one study, more than half of all women of Cuban descent born in the United States had married non-Cubans. And along with assimilation has come a consequence that seems all too typical of American marriages — divorce.

The Greater Cuban Family

Much has been written about the business success of Cuban immigrants. That business success has been due, in part, to the financial involvement of what can be referred

LA CALLE OCHO (EIGHTH STREET)

The advertising world has its Madison Avenue, the business world its Wall Street. Hollywood has Sunset Boulevard. San Francisco has Chinatown, and Los Angeles has East L.A., the center of Mexican American culture in Southern California. Each of these streets or neighborhoods is known for its business, industry, or dominant ethnic group. Eighth Street — Miami's answer to these famous streets — has been the center of what is called Little Havana, the street around which Cuban Americans built their business district and have lived for years. Located here is the memorial to the veterans of the 2506 Brigade, the invasion force that mounted the Bay of Pigs attack.

The signs on the street advertise *cafeterias* (cafeterias or restaurants),

mueblerias (furniture stores), *dulcerias* (bakeries), *seguros* (insurance), you name it. If it's worth owning, you can probably find it on Eighth Street. Here you can walk the street and stop at any of many restaurant windows to drink a *cafecito* (Cuban coffee drunk in miniature cups) and eat an *empanada* (pastry wrapped around meat or tropical fruit). And here you can see the retired Cuban gentlemen in their *guayaberas* (Cuban shirts) settle down for their daily spirited game of dominoes, while listening to the blaring sound of Spanish-language radio over the air. While most of these businesses and restaurants are Cuban owned and frequented by fellow Cubans and other Latin Americans, they also serve as a major attraction for non-Latin Miamians and tourists alike.

A *cafecito* stand is never far away in Miami. This one, on Calle Ocho, comes complete with photo-opportunity board.

to as "the greater Cuban family." That family would consist of fellow Cuban friends and believers who gave of themselves to help other Cubans achieve success.

While most Cubans who arrived in Miami in the early sixties were penniless, a very small number had access to money taken out of Cuba before the revolution. In general, the largest businesses created in Cuban Miami were started by people with business experience in Cuba who had access to this money.

Most of the businesses the exiles created in Miami, though, were small businesses, and these were started with borrowed money. Often this money had been loaned by family members or other Cubans in Miami, since early in the sixties, no American bank would lend money to Cubans. Under the traditional American way of approving bank loans, Cubans held little hope of getting loans.

But what began to happen in Miami was the creation of sort of a *socioismo,* or Cuban "old boys'" network, which also happened to include a number of women. Once these *"socios"* ("business-buddies") enterprises were in place, they would begin to make loans to other Cubans.

These loans would range in amounts from five thousand to thirty thousand dollars and would be offered on the basis of the character, reputation, and business integrity of the borrowers. Often the lenders had known the borrowers in Cuba. Once the new businesses were in operation, they could count on the support of their fellow Cubans, who more often than not preferred to do business in Spanish with Cubans rather than Americans. Many of these businesses were Miami re-creations of the same business back in Cuba.

Creating a New Havana in Miami

It's safe to say that the Cuban Americans who left Miami for points throughout the U.S. and did not return to Miami had for the most part assimilated by the eighties. For these Cuban Americans, the memories of the Cuba they left behind were kept alive by Cuban images in the media, Cuban music, Cuban friends, and, as always, the family. For many of these Cuban Americans, the highlight of every year was the summer trip to Miami to revisit the Mecca of Cuban culture in the United States.

Pepito vividly remembers the summer drives he made to Miami with his parents in the sixties. Not only was he able to see his grandmother and cousins once in Miami, but he was also able to eat the Cuban food and experience the Cuban culture that he dearly loved but was unable to get in the Midwest.

For those who stayed in Miami, though, life in America was much like life in Cuba.

Cuban American seniors enjoy one of Cuba's most popular games — dominoes. This scene is repeated daily at Domino Park on Calle Ocho in Little Havana.

Little Havana incorporates the many faces of Cuban culture in Miami. This wall mural remembers the homeland's Varadero Beach, hailed as one of the most beautiful in the world.

Businesses weren't the only thing re-created in Miami. Also brought to new life were social organizations and even political organizations in exile.

The Politics of Cuban America

The Cubans who came to the States in the early sixties came with the idea that their stay in the United States would only be a temporary one. Politically, they were concerned about the island they had left behind, not about politics on the North American mainland. It's not unusual for immigrant groups who are forced to leave their homelands for political reasons to concern themselves more with matters in the native country than in the United States.

In 1960, most political groups existed mainly to work on anti-Castro activities. On January 23, 1961, a meeting was held in an attempt to organize about sixty of these groups into one that would work toward the overthrow of the Castro regime. But the groups could agree on little except for the fact that Castro should be overthrown. In March, however, the National Revolutionary Council was created with four goals: to overthrow Castro, to hold free elections in Cuba, to return confiscated property back to its owners, and to continue reform in Cuba in a democratic manner.

These efforts culminated in April of 1961 with the botched Bay of Pigs invasion on the southern coast of Cuba. Upon the return of the Bay of Pigs' veterans, most Cubans in Miami turned their political focus toward helping the Cubans who were continuing to arrive and away from activities on the island.

Also in the late seventies, groups of young idealistic Cuban Americans made work visits to the island to help Cuba with its sugar harvests.

Cuban Americans join a group of Nicaraguan exiles during a 1985 march in Miami's Little Havana.

Cuban Americans come together at Miami's Tropical Park in 1986 to welcome home former Cuban political prisoners. Some of them hadn't seen their families in over twenty years.

By 1970, about 25 percent of all Latins living in metropolitan Miami were American citizens, and by 1978, the figure had risen to 43 percent. The majority of those not yet naturalized had begun the naturalization process. This increasing number of Latins (mostly Cubans) becoming citizens was important because it meant that Cubans, as American citizens, now had the right to vote in elections. Cuban Americans were ready to turn their attention to issues affecting them at home — in Miami.

Cubans Come of Age in Miami Politics

In 1980, the Cuban American community was in a state of crisis. This was the year that Miami voters passed what has been referred to as the antibilingual referendum. The referendum, or secret ballot, forbade Dade County officials from giving money to any programs or activities unless they took place in English. This was also a time when the *Miami Herald,* Miami's major newspaper, came under attack for allegedly slanting stories against the Cuban community in Miami, as well as promoting the antibilingual view in the referendum. The antibilingual view, along with the influx of the Marielitos, had created an anti-Cuban sentiment in non-Cuban minds around the city.

Hard times called for hard responses from the Cuban community. Cuban businessmen who had made attempts to integrate themselves into the Anglo community by joining traditionally American business groups took a new look at their positions. They began to work more directly to change public opinions by creating and joining groups such as the Cuban American National Foundation and

Ileana Ros-Lehtinen, shown with her husband, rejoices after becoming the first Cuban American to be elected to the U.S. Congress.

themselves refocusing their attention on their homeland. With the fall of the Soviet Union and the elimination of the huge amount of Soviet aid to Cuba in the late 1980s and early 1990s, Cuba's economy has struggled, leading Cubans in Miami to hope or dream that the situation there could change just as it did in Eastern Europe. This has caused many Miami Cubans to rethink their views regarding Cuba. If political change could come to Eastern Europe without war, then perhaps the same could happen in Cuba. Although public opinion polls reflect that the majority of Cuban Americans would not return to the island to live, there is a feeling that Cuba's brand of government will change and that a dialogue with Cuba may yet be possible.

FACE (Facts about Cuban Exiles) and making plans to support Cuban candidates in local elections. By 1985, Miami had elected its first Cuban American mayor — Xavier Suarez — and other Dade County municipalities had done the same. Hialeah, Sweetwater, West Miami, and Hialeah Gardens — all of these communities elected Cuban mayors. At the beginning of the 1990s, there were ten Cubans in the Florida legislature, and in 1989, Ileana Ros-Lehtinen, a Cuban woman, was elected to the U.S. Congress. In 1993, Lincoln Diaz-Balart, a former Florida state senator, became the second Cuban American elected to Congress.

As Cubans began taking greater care of their political lives in America, they also found

Cuban American Social Organizations

During the early days of exile, Cuban Americans banded together socially for support and for entertainment. As time passed, social organizations were formed to assist incoming Cubans and to promote Cuban culture in Miami. Among them were the *municipios en el exilio* (municipalities in exile) — groups that were designed after their namesake municipalities in Cuba. There were over 120 municipios in Cuba, and they were comparable in size to counties in the United States. In the early sixties, former residents of these municipalities joined together in America to form their own municipios. The primary goal of these groups was to help fellow residents once they arrived in the States. In addition, they worked to foster Cuban culture, traditions, and customs. Most of the municipios published monthly newsletters announcing births, engagements, and obituaries of their residents, in addition to printing photographs of the homeland. Membership in the municipios was open to a broad range of Cubans with differing occupations, ages, and social standing.

Another Cuban American creation in Miami, The Big Five, set out to re-create the atmosphere of the Havana Yacht Club and four similar prestigious and exclusive social clubs in Havana. Other groups such as the Sugar Growers' Association, made up of Cubans who were involved in the business of growing sugar in Cuba, met to keep plans alive for a return to the island.

Finally, Cuban American branches of traditional charitable organizations like the American Cancer Society and the Red Cross worked to raise funds, and other groups, such as the *Amigos Latinoamericanos del Museo*

de Ciencia y Planetarium (Latin American Friends of the Museum of Science and Planetarium) worked to support the arts and sciences in Dade County.

As the Cuban American community and its social and political organizations have continued to multiply in Dade County, the family has also continued to evolve. Cuban Americans, now mainly of the second generation, are continuing to make gains in Dade County. From the Little Havana district surrounding Eighth Street, the Cubans have moved to the suburbs. But while moving toward mainstream America, the Cubans have managed to keep their roots alive, in a city that is headed by a Cuban mayor and is home to more Hispanics than Anglos. On any given weekend, you can find Cuban culture alive and well on the beaches of Key Biscayne and Miami Beach, as Cuban families gather together to swim and sun bathe, listen to music, and eat Cuban food.

The beach still serves as a background for Cuban American families. Here in Miami Beach, friends renew acquaintances.

Stores such as this *botanica* in Miami stock the necessary tools for worshipers of the Afro-Cuban Santería religion. Note both the Christian artifacts and the statues of Santería saints on the top left shelf.

CHAPTER FOUR

RELIGION AND CELEBRATIONS
A BLENDING OF THE FAITHFUL

It was a Catholic priest, Father José Varela, who first voiced the need for Cuban independence from Spain. For his political sins, he was banished from the island and died in Florida in 1853, the year José Martí was born. And it was José Martí, the man who led the Cuban revolutionary effort against the Spaniards in the nineteenth century, who was so revered by the men and women of his nation that he was known as *el apóstol* (the apostle), a term that would suggest he was a deeply religious believer. Ironically, however, Martí was an agnostic, a religious nonbeliever.

Cubans' attachment to religion in general — and especially to Catholicism — has long seemed an awkward mix of devotion and indifference, of faith and doubt. Perhaps it is this apparent blend of contradictory religious impulses that has made Cubans' response to their faith so stormy and yet so personal.

The Church in Cuba

Since Cuba was a colony of deeply Catholic Spain since the time of Columbus, Roman Catholicism obviously became Cuba's primary religion. The Catholic Church was very much a Spanish institution — and a very powerful one at that — until the time of the Cuban revolution in the early 1900s. But once the Cuban republic was born, the Church as an institution lost much of its power in Cuba. It's been estimated that, at the time of Batista's fall from power in the 1950s, 90 percent of all Cubans considered themselves Catholic, but only about 10 percent attended church regularly. Most of those were women.

Other Cubans were Protestants, Jews, and Afro-Cuban believers of Santería — a blend of Catholicism and Afro-Cuban Yoruba religions. Protestantism was introduced to the island in the late nineteenth century and was represented by the Methodist, Presbyterian, and Southern Baptist churches, as well as by several Holiness and Pentecostal sects. There were also a few practicing Jehovah's Witnesses. In all, an estimated 85,000 to 250,000 Protestants lived in Cuba, composed socially of mostly middle- and lower-class Cubans located primarily in urban areas.

Jews have lived in Cuba since the Spanish colonial period, and in 1959 there were five Jewish congregations on the island with a total population numbered at around fifteen thousand. Most of these were Ashkenazic Jews — that is, Jews with ethnic and cultural ties to Central and Eastern Europe. The rest were Sephardic Jews — that is, Jews who traced their origins to the Middle East, Spain, Portugal, North Africa, and other areas around the Mediterranean.

Cubans considered themselves to be religious and spiritual people, but in their own private and personal way. Faithfulness was expressed in personal prayer and worship, unlike the communal approach in most American churches.

Catholicism in Cuba

In 1953, there were 784 registered priests in all of Cuba, roughly one priest for every 7,500 Cubans. In reality, though, there were fewer practicing priests. About-two thirds of all priests were Spanish, and all were educated in Spain. Most churches were located in the city; the few country churches were usually very poor. The Catholic Church in Cuba was not as influential as it was in other parts of Latin America.

But the Catholic clergy and religious orders were heavily involved in education, though religious education was not allowed in Cuban public schools. In Havana, the Jesuits ran the Belén School, while the Christian Brothers, a French order, ran the De La Salle School. Most Cuban parents believed that Catholic schools provided a better education than public schools. In 1946, Cuba's

St. Kieran's in Miami offers a full schedule of Roman Catholic masses in English and Spanish.

only private college was born, the Catholic San Tomas de Villanueva.

At the time of the Castro revolution, almost all of the clergy opposed the Batista regime. They felt as if the revolution might be a solution to the poverty in Cuba and supported Castro almost from the start. By 1961, however, the honeymoon was over, as Castro expelled most Catholic priests from Cuba when he declared the practice of religion illegal. It has been estimated that 135 priests migrated to the U.S., most of them to Miami.

Catholicism in the United States

In the States, the Catholic Church not only offered spiritual support but also assisted in bringing many Cuban children to the U.S. through its *Operación Pedro Pan* program. It also helped relocate immigrants to other parts of the United States.

When they initially arrived in Miami as part of the first wave of immigrants, Cubans looked to the Catholic Church for help in relocating to other parts of the United States and for spiritual guidance. The Catholic Family Organization found sponsorships for many Cuban families with Catholic parishes all around the United States. Typically, that parish would sponsor the family, helping members find jobs and housing while the children enrolled at the parish school. Protestant churches also helped sponsor the relocation of Cuban families.

By the end of 1962, seven parishes in the Miami area had special masses with sermons in Spanish. It was estimated by the Catholic Archdiocese of Miami that the number of baptized Catholics had doubled to more than over three hundred thousand, in large part because of the number of Cuban exiles that had arrived in Miami. In 1964, when the

Catholic Church discontinued its long practice of saying the mass in Latin, the Miami diocese found itself short of Spanish-speaking priests. As a result, a bilingual seminary was started in Miami, which became a model for others around the country. By 1966, there were eight Spanish-speaking priests, with sixteen parishes offering mass in Spanish. Eleven new parishes were established to serve the Cuban refugees.

By 1983, 118 of 610 priests in Greater Miami were Hispanics, including Cuban Auxiliary Bishop Agustin Román. Román was partly responsible for helping subdue an uprising of Cuban prisoners in Georgia in 1987. The prisoners, part of the criminal element who had migrated during the Mariel boatlift, had found out that they would soon be returned to Cuba, and they rioted, taking more than one hundred hostages. The only person the prisoners trusted on the outside was Román, who convinced them to release the hostages. By traveling to Georgia, Román showed the Cuban prisoners that they would not be forgotten by the Church or the Cuban community in Miami.

While immigrant groups in this country are usually expected to learn English and live "the American way," they can generally practice their religion in whatever manner they choose. Cubans were no exception. First-generation Cuban Americans continued to worship in their own private and personal way. It was a rare Cuban American home that didn't display at least a cross or a picture of Jesus Christ. In fact, many Miami back yards featured miniature shrines to beloved Cuban saints such as *La Virgen de la Caridad del Cobre* (Our Lady of Charity), the patron saint of Cuba; *Santa Barbara;* and *San Lazaro* (Saint Lazarus). In Miami, there still exists a public shrine called *Ermita de la Caridad*

Auxiliary Bishop of Miami Agustin Román. Along with most other Cuban priests, he was expelled from Cuba in 1961.

(Our Lady of Charity Chapel), a granite depiction of Our Lady of Charity with arms out-stretched in the direction of Cuba.

Religious Celebrations

Several days throughout the year have special meaning to Cubans. The most significant of these is *La Noche Buena,* or Christmas Eve. The traditional celebration on the island began with dinner featuring *lechon asado* (roasted suckling pig) and *arroz con frijoles negros* (rice and black beans). Later in the evening, the family would attend *Misa de Gallo,* literally the Rooster's Mass but better known as Midnight Mass. That celebration has remained pretty similar in the States. In some Cuban homes, Santa Claus would come to reward the children with presents.

El Dia de los Tres Reyes Magos (Three Kings Day), also known in the U.S. as the Feast of the Epiphany, was traditionally cel-

Worshipers come to the Our Lady of Charity Chapel (*Ermita de la Caridad*) in Miami. Cubans historically have shown great devotion to saints.

ebrated and was the day when families usually exchanged presents. In Miami, a parade on Three Kings Day travels down La Calle Ocho. The parade was started in Miami as a sort of protest against Castro's elimination of Christmas celebrations on the island because they interfered with the sugar harvest.

La Semana Santa (Holy Week) was also widely celebrated in Cuba as a serious religious holiday, as it is in Catholic communities around the world. Palm Sunday, the Sunday before Easter, was a very special day, with many going to church to obtain blessed palms. *Viernes Santo* (Good Friday) was a time for fasting and praying at the stations of the cross, with many processions taking place in the eastern part of the country. The week ended with a deeply religious celebration of Easter Sunday. The celebration has also remained fairly similar in Miami, with the exception of street processions, which generally do not take place in Cuban communities in the States. One other difference between Easter in Cuba and Easter in the States: It's common to see the Easter Bunny in today's Cuban American Easter celebrations, even though Cuban Easter traditionally did not include the Bunny.

Also celebrated every year on September 8 is the feast of Our Lady of Charity, the patron saint of Cuba. In Miami, the holiday is celebrated with a procession that takes place at the Miami Marine Stadium, at the end of which a representation of the saint is brought in by boat, and mass is celebrated.

Other religious holidays of importance to the Cuban community are the feasts of Santa Barbara (Cuba's most revered saint) on

December 4 and All Saints Day on November 1, when all saints are worshiped collectively. Religious celebrations important to the entire family include baptisms and first communions.

The Catholic School

As we mentioned earlier, the Catholic Church in Cuba was widely involved in education. Though many Cuban children from the early waves of migration attended public schools in Miami, the number of Catholic schools has increased dramatically in subsequent years, with enrollment usually at full capacity. Two new high schools for boys and one for girls were established in 1961 and were staffed by priests, brothers, and nuns from Cuba. Miami-area Cuban Americans have continued to argue for the value of a Catholic education. During the 1982-83 school year, Hispanics (mostly Cubans) accounted for more than 65 percent of the more than nineteen thousand students in the thirty primary and eight secondary Catholic schools in and around Miami.

Cuban Americans and the Church in Miami Today

In keeping with general Anglo trends today, Cuban Catholics have shied away from the Catho-

lic Church and are looking to Protestant, Evangelical, and even Santería religions as alternatives. In Miami, nearly thirteen thousand nonpracticing Cubans were visited by the Catholic Church in 1983 as part of the "Third *Encuentro*" (encounter), whose primary goal was to reach out to Hispanics who had stopped practicing.

Those Cuban Americans who continue to practice, however, have made an impact on the Catholic Church. They've been responsible for putting into effect a number of religious programs in the Miami area. Among them are the *Cursillo* (small course), a three-day program of renewal and spiritual discipline that origi-

Conchita Espinosa, founder of the Conchita Espinosa Academy in Havana, recreated the school in Miami. The school's enrollment is 90 percent Cuban American.

BELÉN PREP

Perhaps the best known Catholic school in Miami is the Belén Jesuit Prep School, a recreation of the Cuban school by many of the same Jesuit priests who ran it in Cuba. The school has a rich tradition and history dating back to 1854, when it was created by Royal Charter issued by Spain's Queen Isabella II. In May of 1961, the Castro regime abolished private schools in Cuba, and the school, which Castro himself had graduated from, was seized by military force, and all property was confiscated. Four months later in Miami, the school was established in the United States.

Belén Prep has an enrollment of around eight hundred and classes are held in English. Graduates from Belén have a 100 percent college admittance rate. Its library has more than thirty thousand volumes in both English and Spanish.

nated in Spain. Other religious programs include the Family Encounter Program; the *Camino al Matrimonio,* a marriage preparation program; the confraternities of Our Lady of Charity; the Legion of Mary in Spanish; and the Charismatic Movement in Spanish.

Protestantism and Cubans

During the 1980s, it was estimated that in the United States more than sixty thousand Hispanics a year were converting to Protestantism, and as of 1990, four million out of the twenty million Hispanics in the United States were Protestants. It's tough to tell how many of those Hispanics are Cuban Americans, but one thing is certain — Cuban American Catholics were converting to Prot-

estant and other evangelical religions. It is believed that many Cuban Americans turn to Protestant faiths because of the generally smaller size of the congregations and the smaller and more personalized forms of worship, with which Cuban Americans are very comfortable.

Many Cubans who were practicing Protestants in Cuba have continued to practice their faith in the States. By the early eighties, in Miami alone, researchers had found sixty-seven Hispanic-named non-Catholic churches with Hispanic pastors. Among those were twenty-five Baptist congregations, eleven Assemblies of God, nine Methodist churches, five Pentecostal churches, and twelve churches that represented other religions.

Cuban American Jews

It has been estimated that somewhere between seven thousand and ten thousand Cuban Jews came to the United States from Cuba, most to the Miami area. Some Cuban Jews chose to join American Jewish synagogues, but many of them united to establish a Cuban Hebrew Circle in 1961. The circle, which began mainly as a social gathering, quickly grew to become the Cuban Hebrew Congregation in Miami Beach, an Ashkenazic congregation. Templo Moses, the Sephardic congregation in Miami Beach, is more traditional in religious practice than the Ashkenazic but smaller in size. The division between the two Jewish congregations continues to narrow as the children get to know each other socially and in school. Spanish, not Yiddish, is the language of choice at home.

Temple Beth Shmuel of the Cuban Hebrew Congregation of Miami.

Santería

The most distinctive of the religions practiced by Cubans is Santería. Although this Afro-Cuban religion is most commonly referred to as Santería, it should formally and more respectfully be called *Regla Lucumí* ("Rule of Lucumí"). Regla Lucumí evolved from the religion of the Yoruba and Dahomey slaves that were brought to Cuba from western Africa to work the sugar plantations. To these West Africans, religion was extremely important and revolved around one thought — keeping the gods happy.

The Yoruba people believed that the idea of a God was too large to understand, so they instead chose to consider small parts of the whole God. They felt that God, the Supreme Being, was too distant and thus unable to fulfill the needs of the people. Thus, the Yoruba people paid great tribute to those "small parts of the whole" — the individual *orishas,* or gods, each of whom was responsible for a different aspect of life.

It was thought that by understanding these specialized gods, a better understanding of the whole God could be achieved. Gods had special tastes in beverages and foods; therefore, the sacrifices of drinks and foods to the gods was very important in the religion, as were music and dance.

Practicing Santería in Cuba allowed the displaced Africans a way of retaining their culture, music, and dance, as well as their personality and language. As they were exposed to the Roman Catholic faith along with its symbols and saints, these Afro-Cubans ended up combining two vastly different ideas of religion into one faith that came to be called Santería. And they did so by combining the African concept of gods or orishas

Symbols and graphic representations used in Santería celebrations.

SANTERÍA GODS AND THEIR CATHOLIC SYMBOLS

In Africa, the Yoruba religion embraced hundreds of gods, but in the Afro-Cuban Santería faith, with its roots in the beliefs of the Yoruba, about twenty of these gods are given special attention. They are often associated with images of saints whose statues appear in Catholic churches. Among these gods are the following:

Changó, god of war and thunder, who is closely identified with Santa Barbara, a female saint. Changó sometimes appears as a man and sometimes as a woman.

Ogun, the owner of iron, and *Eleggua,* the messenger of the gods and the master of paths, who are closely related to St. Peter.

Orunmila, the god of wisdom and destiny, who is closely associated with St. Francis. It is believed he had between two hundred and three hundred *Santeros* (Santería priests) in Havana alone looking after his needs.

Olofi, or God, the Supreme Being, who remains at a distance and is out of touch.

---

with the physical symbols of the Catholic religion, particularly the saints, or *santos* — a word with the same root as *Santería.*

Santería also placed great importance and power in magic objects and protective charms. Believers felt that these objects, as well as other powders, herbs, and potions, had great medicinal powers in the hands of the Santería priests, or *Santeros.*

In Cuba, Santería was practiced almost solely by Afro-Cubans. In Miami, though, its practice has crossed racial lines. Throughout the United States in Latino communities, the believers of Santería practice at Santería houses in relative secrecy and under the direction of the Santeros or Santeras. For years, Santería did not enjoy widespread acceptance among non-Afro-Cubans, most of them mainstream Catholics, and so ceremonies were held behind closed doors in private locations. That tradition remains today. There are stores in these communities called *botanicas* that sell objects, good luck charms, and potions used in the practice of Santería.

Santería has also survived in exile. It's hard to tell how many followers of Santería there are in the U.S. We do know, though, that in Miami as in many centers of Latin population and culture, numerous botanicas have popped up to serve believers. It is still a faith practiced primarily by Afro-Cubans, but it has managed to attract a number of new believers, many white ex-Catholics, and other Hispanics who are not Cuban.

Spanish Language in Exile

Just as the Africans were able to retain part of their culture in Cuba, the Cubans have been able to retain their culture in the United States — not only through religious faith but also through the continued use of Spanish in the home and often outside the home. In the next chapter, we'll take a look at Cuban Americans and their use of Spanish in the United States. In Miami, many Cubans who have never learned English manage easily by speaking Spanish only. Unfortunately, however, the price of this form of self-expression by Cuban Americans has been criticism and hostility from non-Cuban groups who feel that Spanish has set Cubans apart from the mainstream of Americans.

A mambo dance group, dressed in traditional garb, performs with accompaniment. Traditional dances and customs are kept alive by folk groups like this one.

CHAPTER FIVE

CUSTOMS, EXPRESSIONS, AND HOSPITALITY
A MATTER OF PRIDE

It was 1963, and Pepito and his family were now in the midwestern United States. Pepito would remember watching his first snowstorm and thinking how strange it was that the rain could come down in frozen form. His family, not used to changes in the seasons, found the winters harsh, the grayness of the days depressing. The climate was different, and life was now played out in a different language. Through it all, however, Pepito and his family continued to speak Spanish at home and eagerly awaited every spring, which would bring back the warmth and signal the coming of summer. The summer trip to Miami would be here soon, and with it would come a return to Little Havana, its music, its food, and its special characters.

In this chapter, we'll look into Cuban Americans' cultural and personal traits. We'll see how Cubans strived to maintain their Cubanness, while at the same time becoming American.

Looking Out for One Another

As we mentioned in Chapter Three, Cuban Americans respect the tradition of the family unit, with 77 percent of all Cuban families consisting of married couples. That respect and desire to care for themselves extends to other Cubans. Pepito recalls his first doctor in the Midwest — Dr. Sanchez, who was beginning his first practice in the United States. He was one of the first Cuban arrivals in the community, and he made his early mark in the area by taking care of Cubans at no charge. This *cariño* (fondness, affection) carries over to life in general for Cubans and has often demonstrated itself in their social gatherings, whether the times be happy or sad.

Pepito's family was met at the airport in Illinois by other Cubans in the community who had heard of their arrival in the local paper. These Cubans became friends of the family, and several of them, still in Illinois, were present at Pepito's father's funeral twenty-eight years later.

Because of their geographical isolation and the natural tendency of immigrants to drift toward people of their own background, it was natural for Cuban Americans to socialize together. This was especially true in communities that, unlike Miami and Union City, didn't have many Cuban American families. These gatherings, held at homes, parks, or beaches, were typically made up of the same ingredients: family and friends, Cuban music, and Cuban food.

These gatherings crossed all social and age lines. Present at these occasions would be kids, parents, and grandparents alike. Upon arrival, a big hug was expected — even between men, along with the customary kiss on the cheek. Kissing on the mouth was considered extremely personal and perhaps even too

This little girl is celebrating her second birthday by trying to knock the candy out of the *piñata* directly overhead.

American. Families came together, anxious to give news of the arrival of relatives and friends in the United States and to share stories of their present experiences with American culture. And always, there was the inevitable discussion about the homeland: Would Castro fall soon? Would the invasion take place by the end of the year? Had so and so gotten out of Cuba yet? The spirit of the day was definitely Cuban, even with casual talk of work and other everyday subjects, such as children and school.

Each family would bring its Cuban records — usually acquired in Miami — along with a dish of food. As long as the necessary ingredients were available, these dishes were usually Cuban. And always, of course, the language of the day was Spanish, spoken as most Cubans do, quickly, loudly, and with accompanying arm gestures, expressive faces, and lots of physical contact — high-spirited cariño at its best. These gatherings of Cubans took place frequently.

As time passed, however, and Cubans continued to assimilate, these gatherings decreased in number. The kids were now older and had their own lives, many with American boyfriends and girlfriends. And the family's circle of friends had grown to include Americans. The support system provided by uniting with friends of the same ethnic background had helped Cuban Americans get through the rough times. Now, many of the parties and gatherings center on a smaller circle of family and close friends.

Today, Cuban Americans still see each other at birthday parties, weddings, graduation parties, and funerals. The cariño demonstrated in those early gatherings remains a Cuban American trait. Time passes, but Cuban Americans still hug, communicate loudly, and remain lifelong friends, even when separated by hundreds of miles.

Expressing Your Cubanness — *En Español*

Your native language is probably the most identifiable part of your culture. If you speak Spanish in an Anglo-American environment,

THE *QUINCEAÑERA*

When Cuban girls turn fifteen, the occasion is celebrated with a *Fiesta de Quince* (fifteenth birthday party), a coming-out party. In Miami, the parties have grown into gaudy affairs staged in ballrooms and costing the families considerable sums of money. The guest of honor wears a formal dress, photos are taken, and lots of people turn out to see the birthday girl make her grand entrance in anything from a horse-drawn carriage to a limo.

it makes you different from those around you. Speaking Spanish may be an important way of keeping your cultural identity strong, but it can also prevent you from assimilating into the dominant culture.

Cubans are intensely proud of their Spanish, and Cuban Americans have continued to speak Spanish at home and even outside the home, especially in Miami. A Latino sociologist whose business takes him to Hispanic communities all over the United States says that Cubans judge other Hispanic Americans by the quality of their Spanish: You must not only speak Spanish but speak it well.

In Miami and Union City, the vast majority of Cuban Americans continue to use Spanish as their primary language, especially in the home. In 1980, before the Mariel migration, the Cuban National Planning Council did a study in Miami and Union City investigating the use of language in thirty-five hundred Cuban American homes. The conclusions were not surprising: 92 percent of Cubans in Miami and 85 percent of Cubans in Union City spoke only Spanish at home. At work, only about 25 percent of those studied spoke mostly or only English.

For Cuban American children, however, the use of language is a bit different. At home they, too, may speak Spanish. But while their parents and grandparents may not be completely proficient in English, more than three-quarters of school-age first-generation and second-generation children consider English

their primary language at school. Most Cuban American children find it easier to communicate with one another and express themselves in English since their Spanish vocabulary is usually not as extensive as their English. This bilingual ability has created a kind of slang that has been termed *Spanglish*. In Spanglish, meeting, instead of the more appropriate *cita,* becomes *mitin;* roast beef becomes *rosbif;* spray becomes *esprey;* and typing becomes *taipin* instead of the traditional *escribir en maquina.*

Gloria Estéfan, the popular Cuban American entertainer from Miami, sings about Spanglish in the chorus of her 1983 song *"Comunicación"* ("Communication"): "If she can't choose between Spanish or English,

Grammy Award-winning Gloria Estéfan is photographed with her star on the Hollywood Walk of Fame.

she'll use both of them at the same time." In the song, Estéfan also uses Spanglish in conversations like this: *"Oye Kiki, quieres ir shopping con nosotros este weekend?"* Kiki replies, *"Mira Gloria, no puedo — tengo que estudiar o me van a flunkear, and anyway, estoy broke."* The conversation roughly translates as "Hey Kiki, do you want to go shopping with us this weekend?" And Kiki replies, "Look Gloria, I can't. I've got to study or I'm going to flunk, and anyway, I'm broke."

Spanglish phrases and puns abound throughout the song. For example, a caller leaving a message on an answering machine says, *"Oye es Marco — llámame para atras."*

The translation, "Hey Marco, call me back," seems straightforward enough, except that here *back* is used in the sense of *behind*. English words transformed into Spanglish include *lunchear* (to go to lunch) and *chequearme* (to get checked out, as by a doctor).

Expressing Culture through the Spanish-Language Media

Whether accepted or not by Miami's English-speaking population, Dade County has become a truly bilingual and bicultural place. Nowhere is this more evident than in Miami's media. Since the early sixties,

BILINGUALISM AND BICULTURALISM IN MIAMI

Because of the increasing number of Spanish speakers moving into the Miami area, the Dade County Commissioners had passed an ordinance in 1973 that officially declared the county bilingual.

In doing so, the county provided government forms as well as a variety of other communications in Spanish and English. And although spoken widely on the streets of Miami, the use of Spanish became a source of resentment for some Anglo Miamians. They felt at a disadvantage in not being bilingual when it came to finding jobs, especially in the service sector.

If, as an English-only speaker, your work put you in contact with the public and much of that public preferred to talk in Spanish, you wouldn't be the best qualified applicant for a job.

These Miamians felt that they shouldn't have to learn Spanish to compete for jobs or to communicate in their own country. By 1980, the backlash against Spanish had

prompted a county-wide antibilingual referendum, or vote, that passed easily, reversing the 1973 ordinance.

The new antibilingual referendum made English the only official language of Dade County. In passing the antibilingual legislation, the Dade County Commissioners gave birth to the English Only movement in the United States. Not surprisingly, bumper stickers with slogans like this began showing up in Miami: "Will the last American to leave Miami please bring the flag?"

Cuban Americans viewed the passing of the antibilingual referendum as an attempt on the part of the Anglo community to put them in their place and silence their growing voice and power. But the passing of the referendum only slowed Miami's movement toward biculturalism. Another study dealing with the use of language in Miami, this time in 1989, showed that the use of Spanish at home and on the job had actually increased.

periodiquitos, or little newspapers, in the form of tabloids and printed in Spanish, have been a staple in Cuban American culture. Three hundred of these newspapers, with patriotic titles such as *La Nacion* (*The Nation*), *Patria* (*Homeland*), and *El Imparcial* (*The Impartial One*), are available in grocery stores and other establishments in and around Little Havana. Many of them speculate about the future of Cuba and keep alive the dream of returning to the island.

El Nuevo Herald is published in Spanish and focuses on issues of concern to Cuban Americans as well as other Latin Americans in Miami.

For many years, *El Diario las Americas* (*America's Daily*) was the accepted Spanish daily in Miami. The paper, which was created in 1953 and is still owned by a Nicaraguan family, is a curious combination of Latin American news and sports and Miami news, often featuring a society page with stories of parties, family anniversaries, birthdays, and *quinceañeras,* the coming-out parties of Cuban American girls celebrating their fifteenth birthdays.

In 1976, however, the *Miami Herald* created a Spanish-language edition of their daily paper called *El Miami Herald.* The decision by the *Herald* to print a Spanish edition was seen by many to be a wise business move, but it also served as a recognition of Miami's dual culture. The fact that the city's most important newspaper saw a need to communicate with its Spanish-speaking population in their native language reflected the growing power of the Cuban American community. The *Herald*'s move was also significant in itself because for many years,

the *Herald* had been accused by many Cuban Americans of not covering the news of their community in a sensitive and unbiased manner. *El Miami Herald* later evolved into *El Nuevo Herald,* an independent Spanish-language edition of the *Herald.*

Radio has been the single biggest way of keeping the Spanish language and the exile mentality alive in Cuban American Miami, which made talk radio popular long before the days of Rush Limbaugh. As of the early nineties, there were still four radio stations, all on the AM dial, transmitting in Spanish and dealing with issues related to Cuba and Cuban Americans in an aggressive and outspoken manner. Two of the most popular are *Radio Mambí* and WQBA, *La Cubanísima* (roughly translated as "The Cubanest"). Spanish-language radio in Miami often expressed anti-Castro views in a passionate and fiery manner, frequently criticizing anyone who dared to express different opinions. The radio station most often expressing politically contrary views, such as establishing a dialogue with Castro, is *Radio Progreso*. The Spanish-language stations have also been a key force behind fundraising efforts to benefit the community in times of need.

Miami is the home of at least two over-the-air Spanish-language television stations. They produce little local programming about Cuban Americans, but they do much to keep alive the use of Spanish in Miami. These stations, affiliated with the two biggest Spanish-language networks — Univisión and Telemundo — are popular in the local Cuban community. Cuban Americans are involved in the management of both networks, and the most popular Spanish-language TV show, *"El Sábado Gigante"* ("Giant Saturday"), is taped in Miami.

Expressing the Culture *con la Música* (with Music)

Along with language, music also helps define the Cuban culture. Mainly dance music, it is the central element of all social gatherings. On cold Saturday mornings in the Midwest, there's nothing that Pepito loves more than cranking up the stereo with the music of current Cuban musicians such as Carlos Varela and Sylvio Rodriguez. Regardless of how cold it is outside, how much snow there may be on the ground, the music makes the house a little part of Cuba — and in doing so helps Pepito keep his Cubanness alive. Whether it be in the Midwest, Union City, or Miami, music is the most practical way that Cuban Americans have of retaining their roots.

Cuban music is a blend of Spanish, African, and Creole rhythms. Instrumentally, it draws from Spanish strings, African drums, and European brass bands. Dating back to colonial times, music served as the background for elegant dinners and events. For the Afro-Cuban slaves, music provided an outlet for practicing their Santería religion, which was heavily based in musical chants and patterns.

Twentieth-century Cuban music builds around a *clave* rhythmic pattern, which one musicologist has explained as a basic one-two / one-two-three or one-two-three / one-two beat, and uses an African-style

Popular talk show hostess Martha Flores of WQBA radio in Miami is on the air.

call and response pattern, where the lead vocalist sings a lyric and is followed by an answering second part. The music also contains a great deal of lyrical improvisation.

Cuban rhythms were the basis for the rumba, mambo, and chachachá, all Cuban dances that, during the thirties, forties, and fifties, were popular in the United States. In the seventies and eighties, salsa music, a hot Latin dance sound predominant in New York, was also very popular in other areas of the country. Many called it modernized Cuban music; in any case, it carried over to Miami.

Cuban kids in traditional garb in the *Paseo* (stroll) part of the annual Calle Ocho Festival.

There, salsa was blended with American popular music and came to be known as the Miami Sound. The most famous practitioners of the Miami Sound are Gloria Estéfan and the Miami Sound Machine. Estéfan's music is bilingual and bicultural and deals with both American and Cuban American themes. Her songs talk about life in the States but also keep alive the memories of the island. In her 1993 Grammy Award-winning release, *"Mi Tierra"* ("My Homeland"), she sings in Spanish, "The land where you were born, you can never forget / Because it holds your roots and everything you left behind."

Other Cuban Americans such as Willy Chirino, Hansel and Raúl, and Carlos Oliva have also been very popular in Miami but have not crossed over to American radio. Their music is mainly in Spanish and also talks about Cuban American life with fre-

quent references to the island. Sociologists have pointed out that traditional Cuban music is played in Cuban American homes not so much because of its popularity but because it helps keep alive the culture along with the ethnic identity. While much of this music has remained within the Cuban American community, Cubans have had a major effect on popular North American music and dance from the 1930s on, as you will read in the next chapter.

The Importance of Being Funny

Most Cubans often use humor to express themselves, often poking fun at themselves to get their point across. There's a common joke in Miami about a scraggly looking dog dragging a leg and looking as if it were just injured in a car accident. He's approached by a pack of bigger, stronger American dogs, with thick, well-kept manes who taunt him for his looks and apparent weakness. The little Cuban dog replies, "Go ahead, laugh. I may look bad now but back in Cuba, I was a German shepherd."

The little dog's pride is similar to that of most Cubans, who view themselves as a proud people in a land of different dogs that perhaps don't understand and appreciate them. They feel they were forced to go to a foreign country without much choice, experienced hard times, and never lost their pride.

That pride, coupled with the accomplishments of the Cuban American community, has contributed to what non-Cubans see as the Cuban trait of self-promotion. In his book *Going to Miami,* David Rieff illustrates this point with the following story: A Cuban film distributor in Miami leads a Cuban friend to believe that he is the fourth-biggest Hispanic film distributor in America. At a party some time later, the Cuban approaches Rieff and tells him about his big-shot friend,

the distributor. When Rieff tells the story to the distributor, the distributor is ecstatic that his friend has already started to spread the news.

The Cuban sense of humor, at times a dark humor, loves to poke fun at today's Cuba. The following joke made the rounds in Miami in the eighties: "Did you hear about Cuba? It's such a vast country that the island is in the Caribbean, its government is in Moscow, its army is in Africa, and its people are in Miami!" The joke referred to the close political ties between Cuba and the Soviet Union and the fact that its troops were in Angola, Africa, fighting in that civil war.

Linking Memories to Cuban Food

In the introduction to her book *Memories of a Cuban Kitchen,* Mary Urrutia-Randelman vividly remembers the foods she ate as a ten-year-old in Havana. To her, as to many Cuban Americans in the States, Cuban food serves as a true reminder and tie to the country they left behind.

In earlier chapters, we spoke about the foods Cubans ate, first in Cuba and then in the States. The Cuban diet has remained relatively intact in spite of the move to the United States. Cuban restaurants are numerous in Miami and, to a lesser degree, in Union City. And the foodstuffs from which Cuban meals are made — vegetable and fruits such as *yuca* (cassava), *frijoles negros* (black beans), *plátanos maduros* (plantains), and papaya — have become readily available in Miami's grocery stores, particularly in the frozen food section.

A typical Cuban meal: (top left) *yuca con mojo* (cassava with sauce); (top right) *mariquitas de plátano* (plantain chips); and (bottom) *arroz con masitas de puerco* (rice with pork cubes). And to drink: Cawy's Materva soft drink. On the lower right is a cup of *cafe cubano* (Cuban espresso coffee).

To help the Cuban American family bring its dinner to the table every night, the tradi-

FLAN DE COCO (COCONUT FLAN)

1 can condensed milk
4 eggs
1 large can shredded coconut in syrup
1 dash vanilla
2 cups sugar

In a small bread mold, heat the sugar and melt into a layer at the bottom of the mold. Allow to cool and harden. Beat the eggs lightly and add the condensed milk and vanilla. Fill the milk can with the coconut in syrup and add to the eggs and milk. Mix well and pour into the caramelized mold. Place the mold in the center of large flat pan containing water so that about an inch and a half of water covers the sides of the bread mold.

Bake at 350 degrees for about one and one-half hours. Cool and refrigerate. Be careful in removing from the bread pan — insert a knife around the edges, perforating the caramel in the mold. Turn the mold upside down on a dish, and the flan should pop out. Serve cold. *Buen provecho* (Good eating!).

tion of the *cantina* has been revived in Miami. The cantina is an old Cuban service, now provided by Cuban American caterers, that allows families to order dinner for the week ahead from a menu. The food is then delivered to your door nightly in stacked metal tins — still hot and ready to eat!

Cuban Hospitality

Maria lives in the same town as Pepito's mom. She has been a friend of the family for many years, has raised several kids of her own, and is now gifted with several grandchildren. But when Pepito comes home to visit his mom, Maria seldom fails to visit, bringing her specially baked treats. This care and thoughtfulness is typical of Cubans, who, day in and day out, confirm that old saying, *"Mi casa es su casa"* ("My home is your home.").

Opening one's home to others is a typical Cuban American quality. American-style invitations were not common in Cuba. Instead, it was common for people to drop in and visit, just as they have continued to do in Miami. When that occurred, *cafecito* (Cuban espresso) was offered instantly, along with something to drink on the side, usually water. The custom of offering cafecitos has carried over to Miami, where a Cuban kitchen is not complete without its own cafecito brewer.

This hospitality also extends to the offering of one's home for other people to stay in. Many immigrants actually lived for a while in other Cubans' homes upon their arrival in the United States. And if one happens to be traveling through a city where Cuban friends live, it would be considered an insult not to expect to spend the night.

Los Atrevidos (The Bold Ones)

As a group, Cuban Americans are friendly and outgoing. They are supportive of one another and welcoming of others. They've been called *atrevidos,* which actually means bold or daring, but which others have interpreted to mean pushy or aggressive. They stay in touch with one another, visit often, and value and respect their parents and grandparents. They treasure their children.

They also value their language and their social gatherings — and they enjoy the company of one another, eating good food, listening to music, and dancing. And most of all, they value their heritage and are proud of being Cuban.

Cuban American swimmer Pablo Morales captured a gold medal in the men's one hundred-meter butterfly competition for the U.S. at the 1992 Olympics in Barcelona. Morales's family left Cuba in the early sixties and went to live in Puerto Rico.

CHAPTER SIX

CONTRIBUTIONS TO AMERICAN CULTURE
MAKING A STATEMENT

From sports to dance, music to education, and fashion to government, Cuban Americans have been leaving their mark on the United States for the last hundred years. Since the early 1960s, they have helped transform Miami into a cosmopolitan, international city that has become the gateway to Latin America. In addition to putting their stamp on Miami, however, over the past century they have made their mark in many fields of endeavor. They started up the cigar manufacturing industry in Florida, gave North American television one of its most beloved performers, and provided American baseball with some of its finest players. They've sent several of their politicians to Congress and even one of their own to the White House to design clothing for a First Lady of the United States.

Cubans Help Develop Key West and Tampa

The Cuban influence on the United States was first felt in Key West, Florida, just ninety miles north of Havana. Years before Miami and Miami Beach were built in the late 1890s, the city of Key West was a thriving center of commerce, much of it built on smuggling and the salvaging of sunken ships. Then the Cubans came. Although Key West was primarily a seaport, it became the center of the U.S. cigar manufacturing industry. The industry was built in the 1870s by Cuban exiles escaping both the repressive Spanish colonists and the high import taxes imposed by the U.S. government on Cuban cigars.

Part of the legacy that these Cuban exiles left behind in Key West was the San Carlos Club, an early gathering spot for Cuban cigar workers and revolutionaries. The San Carlos was also the home of what may have been the first integrated and bilingual school in the United States, where the Black and white children of the cigar workers learned side by side. Originally housed in a wooden structure that was destroyed by fire, the San Carlos was replaced by another building in 1924, and that building was handsomely restored in the early 1990s by Cuban Americans from Miami.

Today, the San Carlos stands on Key West's Duval Street with the shield of the Republic of Cuba on its facade, announcing its proud past and reminding tourists of the country's first sizable Cuban American colony. Fire and labor unrest drove the cigar industry to Tampa. Both the industry and the city prospered, and Tampa eventually became the top manufacturer of cigars in the United States.

Cubans played a large role in the development of Ybor City, the Tampa neighborhood that is today the home of many Cuban Americans — and of the Columbia, one of the finest Cuban restaurants in all of the U.S. Ybor City was named after Vicente Martinez

Ybor, the owner of the biggest cigar factory in Florida. By the late nineteenth century, Cuban Americans, their thriving cigar industry, and their cigars were recognized throughout the United States and around the world.

Present-day Cuban Americans are scattered around the country and live in nearly every state, particularly New York, which had been home to a small Cuban colony in the early 1800. It was in Florida, however, where Cuban American immigrants from the turn of the century, and later those in the 1960s, would make their presence most felt. And it is in South Florida where Cuban Americans as a group have had the biggest impact on American life.

Cuban Americans Transform Miami

There is no other urban center in the U.S. where you can pick up a major daily newspaper and pull out a Spanish-language edition tucked inside. As noted earlier, however, that is the case in Miami, where the *Miami Herald*

CUBAN AMERICANS LEAVE THEIR MARK ON MIAMI

Cuban Americans and their lifestyle have helped give Miami a Latin American feel. Cuban food can be found anywhere in Miami, and the city is home to numerous Spanish-language theaters. Even at Joe Robbie Stadium, the home of the major league Florida Marlins baseball team, you will feel at home if you speak only Spanish.

Many ushers and concession stand workers speak Spanish, Cuban sandwiches are available at the concession stands (right), and the franchise has marketed itself as the team of the Americas. The Marlins have hired a Cuban American Director of Latin American Operations in Tony Perez, the former Cincinnati Reds star. And on its 1994 roster, the team had no fewer than nine Latin American players, including Cuban-born Orestes Destrade. It has the major leagues' only Spanish-language beat writer in Cuban Javier Mota of *El Nuevo Herald* and is one of only three major league teams to broadcast all their games in Spanish on the radio (the others are the Los Angeles Dodgers and the San Diego Padres).

In Miami, the Cubans have also introduced Americans to their food, often at the many Cuban restaurants that dot the

landscape. *Mariquitas* (plantain chips) rest side by side with potato chips at parties, and Cuban sandwiches offer a quick and filling meal. And of course, there's the cafecito, or Cuban espresso, that has become Miami's local drink. From the airport to most street corners, you can get a cafecito just about anywhere in Miami.

Perhaps most importantly, however, the Cubans brought to Miami the entrepreneurial spirit and drive that served as a spark in Miami's economic engine and drove it to become the banking center of Latin America.

publishes its independent daily, *El Nuevo Herald.* By publishing *El Nuevo Herald,* the established *Miami Herald* has signaled Miami Cubans that they are enough of a market to warrant their own newspaper.

It is difficult to find another major U.S. city that is as truly bicultural as Miami or an ethnic group that has developed as extensive a social and economic support network as the Cuban Americans in Miami.

Much has been said and written about the contributions of Cuban Americans to Miami. Many feel that without the entrepreneurial spirit of the Cubans, the recent growth of Miami's economy would have been impossible. All agree that the migration of more than 750,000 Cubans to Dade County has had a tremendous impact on life in South Florida.

Se Habla Español. Most people notice two things about South Florida. One is the amount of Spanish spoken in Dade County; the other is the presence of Cuban culture throughout the area. As discussed in Chapter Five, the city of Miami officially became a bilingual community in the early 1970s, with government forms and communications in both English and Spanish. But in the 1980s, during a time of reaction against bilingualism, the city reversed itself, and English once again became the official language of Miami. This meant that government communications would no longer be published in Spanish and English. As a result of this action, Miami became the seat of the "English Only" movement in this country.

Despite official policy, however, the use of Spanish in South Florida has continued to grow. Cuban Americans, who are now joined in Miami by immigrants from other Latin American countries, support the local affiliates of the two Spanish-language television networks noted earlier: Univisión and Telemundo. Univisión calls itself an American network that speaks Spanish. Its corporate headquarters are in Dade County, and one of its most popular shows is "Cristina," an "Oprah"-like show in Spanish featuring Cuban American host Cristina Saralegui. And like "Oprah," "Cristina" is a show that *se atreve* (dares to) talk publicly of formerly forbidden subjects such as homosexuality and spouse abuse.

Telemundo has a similar show entitled "Cara à Cara" ("Face to Face"), hosted by Cuban American María Lara. Both Univisión and Telemundo are enjoyed by millions of viewers throughout both the United States and Latin America. And back in Miami, as we saw earlier, Spanish-language talk radio continues to thrive.

The face of Cuban America is also represented on Anglo-American network television by personalities like Jackie Nespral, who hosts NBC's weekend "Today" show.

Jackie Nespral of the weekend "Today" show as a nineteen-year-old Orange Bowl queen.

DR. CARLOS FINLAY: MEDICAL HERO

For a good part of the nineteenth century, yellow fever had claimed tens of thousands of lives in many tropical regions of the Americas. Also known as the Black Vomit because of its primary symptom, this killer disease was widespread throughout the Caribbean and in Central America. It even killed people in coastal cities of the United States.

Dr. Carlos Finlay was a Cuban physician who graduated from the Jefferson Medical College of Philadelphia in 1855 at the age of twenty-two. From 1865 to 1881, he wrote ten papers about yellow fever, and in 1881, he proposed that the disease was transmitted by mosquitoes. During the next nineteen years, he was the subject of great criticism from skeptics who disagreed with his hypothesis. But in 1901, Finlay's hypothesis was proven by U.S. physicians working on research in Cuba. In October of 1900, Walter Reed presented a paper that formally accepted Finlay's previously criticized findings. After further experiments in late 1900 and early 1901, Finlay's hypothesis was

further proven. By the end of 1901, the disease had been all but eradicated from Cuba.

Miami Business and Politics. The Cuban business community has played a big role in making Miami a major trader with Latin America. It has been estimated that by the late 1970s, South Florida accounted for 30 percent of all trade with Latin America. And in Miami/Dade, it has been estimated that more than eighteen thousand Cuban-owned businesses have contributed to the local economy.

In recent years, Cuban Americans have also become more and more involved in South Florida politics. By 1994, they had elected Cuban American mayors in five Miami-area communities, including the city of Miami. Cuban-born and Harvard-educated Xavier Suarez was first elected as mayor of Miami in 1985 and with City Manager Rosario Arguelles Kennedy and City Commissioner Joe Carollo formed a majority coalition on Miami's City Commission.

A National Political Force

While becoming a powerful force in South Florida politics, Cuban American citizens — nearly one million strong in the U.S.

Hilario Candela: Surely no other architectural firm in the city has done more work in Miami than Spillis, Candela and Partners.

CUBAN AMERICAN ARCHITECTS: CHANGING THE FACE OF MIAMI

Cuban American architects have changed the skyline of Miami. In the 1960s, during the first wave of immigration, as many as two hundred Cuban architects are thought to have come to the United States.

Cuban architects were involved in many large projects in pre-1961 Havana. The modern style of Cuban architecture was very similiar to that of Miami, and the Cubans were well acquainted with American methods of construction. Cuban architects in South Florida thus had little trouble making it into the local architectural "scene."

Although the famed Arquitectonica firm in Miami was created by a native of Colombia and his American wife, many of its architects are Cuban. The largest architectural firm in Florida — which is also the largest Hispanic architectural firm in the United States — is Spillis, Candela and Partners. This Miami-based firm — one of whose principal partners, Hilario Candela, migrated from Cuba — has been partly responsible for shaping the look and architectural character of the city.

Among the firm's creations are all but one of the Miami Dade Junior College campuses in the Miami area, the City of Miami Convention Center, the Bayside Tourist Center, the Museum Tower, Barnett Bank, and the Southeast Financial Center.

Candela himself has gained some acclaim with his work in designing transitional spaces: the covered spaces, courtyards, and *portales* (porches) that he feels people should pass through before entering Miami's air-conditioned buildings.

as a whole — have also become a key voting block in presidential elections. During the 1988 presidential campaign, for example, George Bush campaigned heavily in South Florida, where his son Jeb headed the Republican party.

In Washington, the Cuban American presence has been felt primarily through the lobbying efforts of the Cuban American National Foundation (CANF) and its point man — the controversial Jorge Más Canosa. Más Canosa is a fiercely anti-Castro Cuban American who has influenced American policy towards Cuba. Through his work with the CANF, Más Canosa has made Cubans a political force to contend with in both foreign and domestic policy.

THE PIONEERING "I LOVE LUCY"

Desi Arnaz, the young Cuban who started out his show business career as the lead singer for Xavier Cugat's Orchestra in the 1940s, married fledgling movie star Lucille Ball. Together they starred in the extremely popular television show "I Love Lucy" and later created Desilu Studios, where the television show was produced.

At Desilu, Desi and Lucy pioneered the present-day form of producing situation comedies on TV — recording in front of studio audiences with multiple cameras. Until that time, television sitcoms had been produced with a single stationary camera, no audience, and artificial laughter known as a "laugh track" or, less formally, "canned laughter."

The Cuban Influence in Music

Of the many success stories about the cultural contributions of Cubans in this country, perhaps none has been as visible as the Cuban impact on American music, which dates back to the early 1930s.

That is when Cuban band leader Don Azpiazu introduced a New York audience to a Latin orchestra with a true rhythm section. And when Azpiazu recorded one of the songs they played, *"El Manicero"* ("The Peanut Vendor"), for RCA, his music soon became a favorite with American audiences nationwide. "El Manicero" touched off what came to be known as the rumba craze, a fad that was named after the Cuban dance. Another Cuban band leader, Xavier Cugat, also enjoyed much success during the rumba craze, play-

Band leader Xavier Cugat helped introduce the rhythms of merengue and rumba to the U.S.

ing nationwide on his own radio show and appearing in several films for MGM. He also introduced a number of young singers who would make a name for themselves, including Frank Sinatra, Bing Crosby, and Cuban-born Desi Arnaz.

Chano Pozo, an African Cuban conga player and composer who was well known in Cuba, came to the States in the late thirties to play with jazzman Dizzy Gillespie's band and had a major influence on Gillespie's work. Gillespie recorded one of Chano's compositions, *"Manteca"* ("Lard"), which some have called the greatest Afro-Cuban work of all time.

During the forties and fifties, the Cuban influence on American popular culture was at its peak. The mambo and the chachachá (both Cuban dances) became popular in the States, and conga lines were forming everywhere, thanks to Cuban-born Machito (Frank Grillo) and his Afro-Cubans, and Pérez Prado and his orchestra.

African Cuban *tumbadores* (conga players) also left their mark on American music. Mongo Santamaria was successful with his Latin jazz groups on the West Coast, and Armando Pereira fueled the hot sounds of such early Santana records as "Evil Ways," "Oye Como Va," and "Black Magic Woman."

Salsa, the Latin dance sound popular in the seventies and eighties, featured among others Cuban singer Celia Cruz. As we learned in Chapter Five, salsa traveled from New York to other areas of the nation, including Miami, where Cuban American mu-

Cuban American singing sensation Jon Secada holds his 1993 Grammy Award for the best Latin Pop Album — *Otro Día Más Sin Verte* (*Another Day Without Seeing You*).

sicians took it under their wing, blended it with American popular music, and created the Miami Sound. Gloria Estéfan and the Miami Sound Machine, in addition to making the Miami Sound a big hit throughout the nation, also spawned the career of Jon Secada. Secada started out as a background vocalist for Estéfan and in 1992 released a successful debut album that received heavy air play on radio stations across the country and produced several hit singles.

In addition to being a player in the major leagues, Miguel Angel Gonzalez was also a coach on the famous St. Louis Cardinal Gashouse Gang teams of the 1940s.

Tony Oliva, the 1971 American League batting champion, shares a family reunion in Mexico with his sister and father. When they met here, they had not seen each other in eleven years.

Cuban Americans and the National Pastime

North American baseball fans are well aware of the adventures and performances of 1990s Cuban American major league stars José Canseco and Rafael Palmeiro. And to a lesser degree, the story of pitcher René Arocha has been told — how he defected from the Cuban national team in the early 1990s and had an outstanding season with the 1993 St. Louis Cardinals.

But Cuban *peloteros* (baseball players) figured in the early history of both major league baseball and the African American Negro Leagues, where American baseball's color line segregated all players of African descent, Cuban and American alike.

The first Latin American ballplayer to play in the major leagues was Esteban Bellan, a Cuban who donned the uniform of the Troy, New York, Haymakers of the National Association of Professional Baseball Players for the 1871 season. The Association would later become the National League. Bellan later returned to Cuba, where he played a major role in developing the game on a professional level on the island.

Other Cubans who distinguished themselves in the American majors included pitcher Adolfo Luque, who won twenty-seven games in 1923 with the Cincinnati Reds, and Miguel Angel Gonzales, who at about the same time was beginning a seventeen-year career in the majors, after which he would become a coach. Baseball lore has it that the term "good field, no hit" was coined by Gonzales after completing a scouting report on an opposing team. It

Outfielder José Canseco slugged 231 home runs in his first eight years in the majors. A street in Miami has been named after him.

is still used to refer to players who have excellent fielding skills but are poor hitters.

The only Cuban player who was honored by induction to the baseball Hall of Fame at Cooperstown, New York, was Martín Dihigo, an African Cuban who first came to play ball in the States as a fifteen-year-old. Dihigo was considered to be one of the most versatile baseball players ever to play the game and starred with a number of Negro League teams in the United States. During the Cuban winter seasons, Dihigo starred in exhibitions against visiting American major league teams. He later managed in Mexico, where he was inducted into the Mexican Hall of Fame. He was also honored with induction into the Venezuelan Hall of Fame.

Other Cuban Americans who distinguished themselves in the majors were the Chicago White Sox's Orestes Minnie Miñoso,

Tony Perez, the top RBI man in the big leagues from 1967 to 1976. He later became the Florida Marlins' Director of Latin American Operations.

Alberto Salazar, shown here crossing the finish line, was a prominent track star in the 1980s, winning both the New York and Boston marathons (1982) and earning spots on two U.S. Olympic teams (1980 and 1984).

the first African Cuban player to hit the big leagues; Minnesota Twins' outfielder Tony Oliva; Baltimore Orioles' pitcher Mike Cuellar; and Boston Red Sox's pitcher Luis Tiant, whose father had also played in the Negro Leagues. Infielder Tony Perez, now in the Florida Marlins' front office, starred with the powerhouse Big Red Machine teams of Cincinnati in the 1970s. Cuban American Preston Gomez was the majors' first Hispanic manager when he guided the Houston Astros in the 1970s.

ROBERTO GOIZUETA — THE REAL THING

It seems most appropriate that the Coca-Cola Company, producer of soft drinks for the world, should have foreign-born Cuban American Roberto Goizueta as its chief executive officer.

Goizueta started his career with Coke as a chemist with the Coca-Cola bottling plant in Havana after having graduated from Yale University in 1953. He left Cuba in the early 1960s to work for Coca-Cola in Nassau, Bahamas, where he rose through the corporate ranks and in 1964 was named assistant vice-president of research. In 1981 he was named chief executive officer and later company president. Goizueta has also served on the boards of the Ford Motor Company and Eastman Kodak.

Several second-generation Cuban Americans appeared in the majors in the early 1990s. The most notable of those were the New York Yankees' Danny Tartabull, the son of José Tartabull, who played with several big league teams in the 1960s; and the California Angels' Eduardo Perez, Tony's son.

In the world of track and field, marathoner Alberto Salazar etched his name in the record books by winning the 1982 New York and Boston marathons. Salazar had been named to the 1980 U.S. Olympic team that boycotted the games in Moscow, but he was able to represent the U.S. at the 1984 Olympics in Los Angeles, where he finished out of medal contention.

Cuban Americans in Books and the Movies

Writing in their native Spanish about mostly political themes, the first Cuban American writers quietly but powerfully expressed the serious feelings they had upon leaving their beloved island to live in a foreign culture.

These Cuban American writers — those who came in the early 1960s — talked about both the injustices they faced in Cuba and the beauty of the land they left behind. They also expressed the uneasiness of feeling neither Cuban nor American, yet having no choice but to stay in the United States. Ironically, they were not the first Cuban American writers to face this situation. In the late 1800s, José Martí, the Cuban poet who was at the forefront of the Cuban revolution, had made his living as a writer while living in exile in New York.

Books such as *Enterrado Vivo* (*Buried Alive*), by Andrés Collado, and *Tres Tristes Tigres* (*Three Sad Tigers*), by Gabriel Cabrera Infante, talked about life in Fidel Castro's

Cuba Roja (*Red Cuba*) and other books about Cuba and by Cuban Americans abound on this table at the Books and Books store in Coral Gables.

Cuba and about Cubans in Miami. And Lydia Cabrera, whose career was dedicated to telling the story of the African Cuban folk tradition, wrote a great deal about the African Cuban Santería religion. Her collection of nineteen Afro-Cuban short stories, *Ayapá: Cuentos de Jicotea* (*Ayapá: Tales of a Turtle*), was published in the United States in 1971.

Poetry and the short story have always been an important part of the Cuban literary tradition. Cuban writers, many of them serving prison sentences in their homeland for antirevolutionary activities, have produced volumes of political verse, most of it under-standably expressing anti-Castro sentiments. Among these were Heberto Padilla, who came to Miami in 1980 after serving time in Cuban prisons, and Armando Valladares, who also came to the U.S. after becoming disenchanted with the Cuban revolution.

Reinaldo Arenas came to the U.S. from Cuba during the Mariel boatlift. A homosexual with AIDS, Arenas committed suicide in 1990 in New York after publishing his memoirs, *Before Night Falls.* In this book, Arenas sensitively tells the story of the persecution he and other homosexuals have suffered in Cuba today.

CUBAN AMERICAN WOMEN: SOME SUCCESS STORIES

Upon their arrival in the United States in the early 1960s, many Cuban American women found it easier to find work than their male counterparts. Many women were more apt to perform menial labor than Cuban men, particularly in businesses like the garment industry. As a result, many women entered the workforce to support their families while men looked for work, and once they were employed, they never stopped working, even when the men found jobs. Other women resumed in the U.S. the careers they had started in Cuba.

In the world of politics, Miami's Ileana Ros-Lehtinen was elected to the House of Representatives in 1989, while Rosario Kennedy has served as Miami city manager and Miriam Alonso has served as vice mayor.

Social activist Graciela Beecher operates the Cuban-American Legal Defense and Education Fund in Fort Wayne, Indiana, while Maria de los Angeles Torres is a professor at DePaul University in Chicago. Also at DePaul is Professor Pastora San Juan Cafferty, who was born in Cuba and educated in the U.S. Cafferty served as assistant to both the secretary of Transportation and the secretary of Housing and Urban Development in the late 1960s. Another Cuban American public servant is Cari Dominguez, who was named by President Bush as the director of the Office of Federal Contract Compliance Programs.

Gloria Estéfan won a Grammy in 1993 and is among the country's top female vocalists. Maria Irenes Fornés is considered the dean of Hispanic playwrights and has won six Obie Awards for her work in the theater.

In the business world, Remedios Diaz-Oliver has built up a glass and plastic bottle supply company and started another successful container company in Miami, while another entrepreneur, Teresa Zubizarreta, established a successful Miami advertising business.

Fernando Bujones danced with the American Ballet Theater in the 1980s.

Other writers, like Celedeno Gonzales, have concentrated on living in exile in the United States and on the culture shock that comes from the conflict between Cuban and American life. As time has passed, however, Cuban American writers have dealt more and more with the present-day concerns of the Cuban American community as well as with more poetic subjects, such as the authors' memories and dreams.

Such is the case with the works of Oscar Hijuelos, the son of working-class Cubans who immigrated to the United States in the forties. New York raised and educated, Hijuelos became, in 1990, the first Hispanic writer to win a Pulitzer Prize, for *The Mambo Kings Play Songs of Love,* upon which the movie *The Mambo Kings* was based. His book follows the adventures of the fictional Castillo brothers, who come to New York from Cuba looking for musical stardom. Having been born in New York, Hijuelos has talked about his Americanization and how his artistic expression has allowed him to retain his ethnic identity without ever having set foot in Cuba.

Cristina Garcia, a Cuban American writer who was born in Havana, has also given us a portrayal of Cuban characters in her critically acclaimed novel of 1992, *Dreaming in Cuban.* In her first book, Garcia sends the reader back and forth from Brooklyn to Havana, as she takes a look at four women of the Del Pino family.

A Cuban American who has drawn critical acclaim for his work in the movies is actor Andy Garcia, who was born in Havana and came to the States as a child. Most noted for his performances with Kevin Costner in the film version of *The Untouchables,* with Al Pacino in *Godfather 3,* and with Meg Ryan in *When a Man Loves a Woman,* Garcia has had a productive career since his first motion picture in 1983.

Looking Forward

Beyond the glamor of stars like Gloria Estéfan, Jon Secada, Andy Garcia, José Canseco, and ballet dancer Fernando Bujones, there are countless other Cuban Americans about whom we haven't heard. The thousands of teachers, factory workers, garment workers, restaurateurs, judges, lawyers, doctors, chemists, video producers, and politicians — as well as wives and mothers and husbands and fathers — toil in anonymity, going about their daily tasks with a self-confidence that is both Cuban and American in nature.

As we approach the turn of the century, the first generation of Cuban Americans — those who made up the first wave of immigrants — will be aging, and many Cuban American "baby boomers" will be ready to retire. In places like Miami and Union City, the Cuban legacy will continue, but with an American twist. While the experts debate whether coming genera-tions of Cuban Americans will continue to speak Spanish, there is evidence today that the third generation of Cuban Americans already considers English their primary language and the United States their country of choice.

What began as a "temporary" stay in the United States has turned into a lasting existence for all Cuban Americans. The Cuban influence in Miami has given the city a Latin American feel, perhaps as it might have been if Havana had continued as a haven for tourists and big business from throughout the Americas.

In any case, it appears that Cuban assimilation into American life is continuing at a normal pace for a group of recent immigrants. Pepito's second cousins in Miami aren't as interested in celebrating *quinceañeras* as past generations were, but they suggest to their mom other, more American ways of celebrating a teenager's fifteenth birthday. And just like other American teenagers, Cuban American teens like to hang out at the "Grove" (Coconut Grove). Our Cuban roots may grow deeper, but we cannot separate ourselves from the American soil in which they grow.

Pepito remains in the Midwest — listening to the music of Silvio Rodriguez, Carlos Varela, and Los Van Van, peering out into the snow-covered ground on cold winter mornings, wondering if he'll get to visit Cuba again.

Los Cubanos continue to strive toward the American dream of success, prosperity, and happiness, but in their own Cuban American style. Stay tuned.

Chronology

1848 U.S. President James Polk offers Spain $100 million dollars to purchase Cuba; Spain rejects the offer.

1868 Oct. 10: Cuba's Ten-Year War, or First War of Independence, begins when Cuban sugar planter Carlos Manuel de Céspedes frees his slaves and issues a declaration that comes to be known as *El Grito de Yara* (the Yara Shout).

1871 Cuban Esteban Bellan becomes the first Latin American major league baseball player in the National Association of Professional Baseball Players.

1878 February: Cuba's Ten-Year War ends with the Pact of Zanjon as Cuban rebels reluctantly come to settlement with Spanish authorities on the island.

1895 Cuba's Second War of Independence begins; in the spring, revolutionary leader José Martí dies in battle.

1898 Feb. 15: U.S. battleship *Maine* blows up in Havana harbor, killing 260 crew members; April 20: U.S. declares war on Spain, beginning the Spanish-American War; Dec. 10: Spanish-American War ends; peace treaty is signed ending Spanish domination of Cuba, Puerto Rico, and the Philippines. U.S. military government in Cuba is put in place.

1900 Cuban doctor Carlos Finlay's theory for transmission of yellow fever is accepted by U.S. doctor Walter Reed; one year later, yellow fever is wiped out in Cuba.

1901 May 28: the Cuban Constitutional Convention adopts the U.S.-mandated Platt Amendment to the Cuban Constitution, giving the U.S. the right to intervene in Cuban affairs in order to maintain a government that will protect Cuban lives, property, and individual liberties.

1902 20 May: Tomás Estrada Palma is inaugurated as the first president of Cuba; the Cuban flag flies atop the Morro Castle in Havana.

1906 President Tomás Palma resigns, Americans begin twenty-six months of rule by decree.

1912 Revolt in Oriente prompts the United States to send Marines to Cuba.

1917 Another revolt prompts the landing of U.S. Marines once again.

1923 Cuban pitcher Adolfo Luque wins twenty-seven games for the National League Cincinnati Reds.

1933 August 12: rule of General Gerardo Machado (1925-1933) comes to an end when the army drives him out of the country; Machado flies to Nassau; many of his supporters end up in Miami, where Machado is eventually buried; Sept. 4: group of army sergeants led by Fulgencio Batista takes power, overthrowing Machado's successors; Batista will remain as a powerful political figure in the military.

1934 May: U.S. cancels the Platt Amendment; Cuba is now truly independent.

1952 March 10: military, led by Fulgencio Batista, drives President Carlos Prío Socarras out of Cuba to Mexico and eventually to Miami; military rule returns to Cuba.

1958 Dec. 31: Batista quits, fleeing the country; Fidel Castro takes control of the island; Cuban migration to the U.S. begins.

1960 July 5: Cuban Council of Ministers authorizes the seizure of all U.S. property in Cuba; first wave of Cuban migration continues, with over 280,000 Cubans leaving the island from 1960 to 1962.

1961 President Kennedy establishes the Cuban Refugee Program; April 17: the U.S.-sponsored 2506 Brigade of Cuban exiles lands at Playa Girón, Cuba; the Bay of Pigs invasion begins.

1962 October 22: President Kennedy imposes a naval blockade on Cuba, preventing Soviet missiles from entering Cuba; this event comes to be known as the Cuban Missile Crisis; the first wave of Cuban migration ends as Cuba suspends travel to the U.S.

1965	September: Cuban government opens the port of Camarioca to exiles wanting to pick up relatives from Cuba; five thousand Cubans leave Cuba; the second wave of Cuban migration is underway; December: two daily flights from Varadero Beach, Cuba, begin to fly Cubans to the U.S.; between 1965 and April 1973, when the flights are stopped, about 280,000 Cubans arrive in the U.S.
1973	Dade County, Florida, Commissioners declare the county officially bilingual.
1980	April 1: Cubans seeking to leave the country crash into the Peruvian Embassy in Havana; events set off the great boatlift at the port of Mariel; April 20: first boats from Mariel arrive in Key West; third wave of Migration is underway; by September, it is estimated that about 125,000 Cubans have left the island; antibilingual referendum passes in Miami.
1982	Martín Díhigo is voted into the Baseball Hall of Fame in Cooperstown, N.Y.
1985	Xavier Suarez is elected as first Cuban-born mayor of Miami.
1989	Ileana Ros-Lehtinen is elected as first Cuban-born representative to U.S. Congress.
1993	Cuban-born Lincoln Diaz-Balart is elected to Congress; Gloria Estéfan wins a Grammy for "Mi Tierra."
1994	August: *Balseros* (rafters) leave Cuba by the thousands in hopes of reaching Florida; in an effort to force the U.S. to discuss Cuban-U.S. relations, Fidel Castro refuses to restrict this latest wave of exiles; this creates an immigration and diplomatic crisis for the U.S., which reverses its longstanding policy of granting asylum to all Cuban exiles and placesCuban refugees in detention centers outside the nation.

GLOSSARY

Assimilation	Becoming similiar to others within a culture or community.
Asylum	Protection given by a country to a political refugee of another country.
Batistianos	Followers of Fulgencio Batista, former president of Cuba.
Bay of Pigs	Bay on the southern coast of Cuba, where the invasion of Cuba by the 2506 Brigade, a group trained and supported by the U.S. government, took place in an effort to overthrow the government of Fidel Castro.
Botanica	A store where spiritual and religious symbols used in Santería are sold.
Cosmopolitan	Worldly or sophisticated.
Cubanness	A sense of Cuban identity; pride in being Cuban.
Cuban Missile Crisis	Face-off between the United States and the Soviet Union in 1961. U.S. military ships kept Soviet ships from delivering missiles to Cuba.
Cuban Winter League	Integrated baseball league that played its games during the winter in Cuba. Many American players played in this league, particularly African Americans who were kept out of the segregated U.S. major leagues.
Culturally diverse	(Usually a community or nation) containing or representing people with backgrounds from different countries and cultures.
Defection	Escaping from a country.
Emigré	A person fleeing his or her own country, usually because of political conditions.

Entrenched	Placed in a position of strength; firmly situated.
Entrepreneur	An independent business person not afraid to take financial risks.
Exodus	The departure of a large number of people.
Grandes Ligas	The U.S. big leagues; baseball's major leagues.
Idealistic	Believing in things as they should or could be instead of as they are.
Literacy rate	The number or percentage of people able to read and write.
Machismo	Latin American male behavior and attitude, often equated with male chauvinism or with a superior role of the male in the family.
Mainstream	The principal trend, course, or culture of a group or community.
Marielitos	Cubans who left Cuba in 1980 from the port of the Cuban city of Mariel.
Naturalization	The act of becoming a citizen of the United States.
Patriarch	A male head of a family.
Plantain	A tropical fruit resembling a banana; used primarily for cooking.
Regla Lucumí	Yoruban religion from which Santería developed.
"Se Habla Espanol"	Spanish for "Spanish Spoken Here."
Sierra Maestra	Range of mountains in eastern Cuba where Fidel Castro began his revolutionary fight.
Socialist	One who is a believer in socialism, a method of social organization that promotes ownership and control of property by the community as a whole.
Sponsorship	The act of being financially responsible for a person or thing.
2506 Brigade	The group of men, primarily Cuban, who took part in the Bay of Pigs invasion.

FURTHER READING

Allman, T.D. *Miami, City of the Future.* New York: The Atlanta Monthly Press, 1987.

Bethell, Leslie, ed. *Cuba: A Short History.* New York: Cambridge University Press, 1993.

Cortino, Rudolfo, ed. *Cuban American Theater.* Houston: Arte Publico Press, 1991.

Grenier, Guillermo J., and Stepick, Alex, eds. *Miami Now! Immigration, Ethnicity and Social Change.* Gainesville and Tallahassee: University Press of Florida, 1992.

Kanellos, Nicholas, ed. *The Hispanic-American Almanac: A Reference Work on Hispanics in the United States.* Detroit: Gale Research, 1993.

Masud-Piloto, Felix Roberto. *With Open Arms: Cuban Migration to the United States.* Totowa, N.J.: Rowman and Littlefield Publishers, 1988.

Portes, Alejandro, and Stepick, Alex. *City on the Edge: The Transformation of Miami.* Berkeley and Los Angeles: University of California Press, 1993.

Rieff, David. *The Exile: Cuba in the Heart of Miami.* New York: Simon and Schuster, 1993.

Rieff, David. *Going to Miami: Exiles, Tourists and Refugees in the New America.* Boston and Toronto: Little, Brown and Company, 1988.

Shorris, Earl. *Latinos: A Biography of the People.* New York: Avon Books, 1992.

Urrutia-Randelman, Mary, and Schwartz, Joan. *Memories of a Cuban Kitchen.* New York: MacMillan, 1992.

INDEX

NATIONAL UNIVERSITY
LIBRARY

DATE DUE			
APR 1 5 2003			
JUN 1 1 2003			

GAYLORD M2